# The
# Information
# Society

# THE
# INFORMATION
# SOCIETY

## An International
## Perspective

RAUL LUCIANO KATZ

**PRAEGER**

New York
Westport, Connecticut
London

**Library of Congress Cataloging-in-Publication Data**

Katz, Raul Luciano.
  The information society.

  Bibliography: p.
  Includes index.
  1. Information technology—Economic aspects—Developing
countries.  I. Title.
HD9696.A3D446      1988      338.4′7004′091724      87-25884
ISBN 0-275-92659-1  (alk. paper)

Library of Congress Catalog Card Number: 87-25884
ISBN: 0-275-92659-1

First published in 1988

Praeger Publishers, One Madison Avenue, New York, NY 10010
A division of Greenwood Press, Inc.

Printed in the United States of America

∞

The paper used in this book complies with the
Permanent Paper Standard issued by the National
Information Standards Organization (Z39.48-1984).

10  9  8  7  6  5  4  3  2  1

# Contents

**GENERAL CONCLUSION**                                                      **131**

# List of Tables

# List of Figures

# Acknowledgments

Many persons contributed in different ways to this study. As my advisor and teacher, the late Ithiel de Sola Pool was the principal force guiding both my coursework and research at M.I.T. He supervised my master's thesis, and reviewed earlier drafts of the dissertation that served as a basis for this book. Many of the ideas presented in this work—as well as the approach toward data analysis and theory formulation—are greatly influenced by his supervision throughout my four years at M.I.T.

Many other members of the M.I.T. faculty contributed with insightful comments, both in terms of the content and structure of this study. Russell Newman from the Political Science Department and Michael Scott Morton and Charles Jonscher from the Sloan School of Management continuously obliged me to seek clarity in the presentation, and provided me with key comments that challenged some rapidly drawn conclusions.

In an indirect way, many others contributed to shaping my views on the interaction between politics and information technologies.

I would like to thank Beatrice Sikon and Stanley Schrager—both Vice-Presidents of the Chase Manhattan Bank—who were instrumental in obtaining financial support for completing the dissertation.

Joseph Mallory—Senior Vice-President at Booz, Allen & Hamilton—arranged for production support of the final manuscript. I would like to thank Sarah O'Reilly, Kevin Bartley, and the staff of Central Report Production at the New York office of Booz, Allen & Hamilton, for their contribution in the preparation of the final manuscript.

In a very special way, I would like to thank my wife, Barbara C. Samuels—whom I met at M.I.T., and with whom I have shared seven years of intellectual enrichment. Her encouragement and dedication in reviewing many drafts of this book have been a major contribution.

# Introduction: Politics and the Information Society

The term "information society" has been used to describe socioeconomic systems that exhibit high employment of information-related occupations and wide diffusion of information technologies.[1] The growth in demand for information workers and the rapid diffusion of information technologies have been identified and studied mainly in the case of developed countries.[2] Several developing countries are also starting to show—at least partially—the key traits of an information society.[3] In spite of this, research on the analysis and explanation of this trend among developing countries is rather scarce. Furthermore, the information societies emerging in the developed and developing worlds have not been compared.[4] This book attempts to partially fill these gaps.

The book analyzes four questions: First, is there a universal process of emergence of a sizable information sector in the workforce structure across countries, particularly in the developing world? Second, is there a similarity in the internal structure of the information sector in different countries? Third, are there any universal trends in the process of diffusion of information technologies on a worldwide level? And fourth, if the response to any of the first three questions is negative, what are the factors causing different evolutionary paths and distinct profiles of information societies?

The approach taken in this study rests on two related assumptions that implicitly underlie all of the four above questions. First, no one model of an information society encompasses all countries. Second, the way in which information societies develop—the growth in demand for information workers and the diffusion of information technologies—is neither universal nor unilinear.

If these assumptions are true, not only do divergent transition processes exist, but also different models of the information society. This idea was originally raised by Daniel Bell (1973), when he questioned the possibility of uniform development paths toward postindustrial stages.[5] Based on Bell's proposition, this study is structured around the notion of diverse development processes leading to information societies that are also diverse.

In explaining the development pattern of information societies in industrialized countries, authors such as Porat (1977), Barnes and Lamberton (1976), and Jonscher (1982a) have shown that the expansion of the employment share of information occupations and the diffusion of information technologies are determined mainly by the need to promote greater efficiency in the production of goods and services.

This study proves that—contrary to what happens in industrialized countries, where the economy seems to be the main explanatory variable—in developing countries, politics are the decisive variable in driving the transition to information societies. This hypothesis is comprised of two subhypotheses.

The first one is that the increase in demand for information workers in many developing countries is due more to the growth of the government than to the expansion of the private manufacturing and service sectors of the economy. In most developing countries, the initial growth of the share of information employment is partially due to the slower growth of total factor productivity in services, as compared to manufacturing.[6] In addition, the increase in the share of information occupations in the developing world is also the result of dysfunctional education systems, generating a surplus of educated labor force relative to employment opportunities in the economy.[7] Within this context of an oversupply of information workers, the government acts as a compensating mechanism on two levels: First, state and local governments tend to grow in order to partially counter rural-urban migration. Second, the central government often grows beyond its needs in order to absorb the increased supply of information workers, and thereby reduce the potential for political opposition due to unemployment.

The second subhypothesis argues that, if put in Lindblom's terms, it is politics—rather than markets—that drives the diffusion of information technologies in developing countries. Despite the existence of certain elements of competition, the international market for information technologies is hardly efficient. As a result, whether an information technology is adopted or not by a country is largely determined by its internal patterns of power, influence, and resource allocation policies—as well as the relation of political interdependencies at a worldwide level. This is not a new assertion. However, this book provides systematic and quantitative evidence for an argument that, until now, has been mainly supported by anecdotes and scattered findings.

In sum, this study supports the notion that the growth in demand for information workers and the accelerated diffusion of information technologies in developing countries respond to a set of factors, among which the need for managerial efficiency in the production of goods and services plays a secondary role.[8] Contrary to this, the emergence of an information society in most developing countries is extensively related to the growing needs of governments involved in the process of developing the material capacity to control, extract, and allocate societal resources within their populations and territories.

In proving these hypotheses, this study encompasses more than a restatement of the theory of information societies. By highlighting the importance of political factors within a positivistic framework, it challenges the conventional normative approaches, which consider the development of societal communications systems to be the result of the socioeconomic transformations associated with the modernization process.

The introduction of political variables in the analysis of the information society has a second theoretical implication. As Nordlinger states, the introduction of the political variable

involves the raising of fundamental questions about the sufficiency and relative importance of the alternative, society-centered focus, along with the more or less tentative introduction of propositions that run directly counter to social and economic determinism. (Nordlinger 1984, 2)

It is argued throughout this study that, in past years, the emergence of information societies has been almost exclusively related to socioeconomic factors—avoiding direct reference to political variables, such as the role of the state.[9]

From a theoretical standpoint, this study is related to the pioneering work of Karl Deutsch on the interaction between information technologies and political systems.[10] In addition, research on the social characteristics of information societies in developed countries[11] has greatly influenced the definition of this study's main assumptions.

Four approaches have been utilized for measuring the scope of the "information society." The first approach has been the analysis of the structure of employment. It proceeds by isolation the information-related or "knowledge-based" occupations from the service, industrial, and agricultural workforces (Machlup 1962; Porat 1977; OECD 1981). The second approach consists of analyzing the intracountry diffusion of information technologies (Frey 1973; Cruise O'Brien et al. 1977). The third approach has been the study of the contribution of the information sector to the gross product of domestic economies. In this case, data is derived from either national accounts or input-output tables (Porat 1977; OECD 1981; Jussawalla and Chee-Wah-Cheah 1982). The fourth approach analyzes information flows by measuring the number of words transmitted by major information technologies and "consumed" by the population of a given county (Tomita 1975; Pool et al. 1984). The present study utilizes the first two approaches outlined above, and explores the influence of the political variable on each of them.

Part I focuses on the analysis of the workforce structure: the first chapter presenting empirical data, the second chapter introducing a model of causality. We then explore the changes occurring within the workforce structure of selected countries. By analyzing the internal structure of the information sector in various developing countries, the key role played by the government in driving sector expansion is shown. First, data show that the information workers' share of the economically active population in all developing countries is increasing, regardless of the countries' rate of industrialization. This is an indication that factors other than specialization and division of labor are causing the information workforce to grow. Second, the profile or internal structure of a country's information workforce is shown to vary. Two countries may have the same proportion of their labor force employed in information-related occupations; but one of the countries exhibits a major share of information workers working in government, while the second country features a strong private-sector share. Third, the study shows that the lower the level of economic development of a country, the higher the government workers' share of the total information workforce. Finally, building on the evidence, a model that includes the multiple variables driving the growth of the information workforce is presented.

Part II focuses on the diffusion of information technologies, first reviewing the research literature, and then defining a general causality model, which emphasizes the role of political variables. The rest of Part II presents empirical evidence supporting our general causality model. First, the study shows how mail and telephone tariffs—set by governments—have a decisive impact on the process of substitution between different point-to-point information technologies. Second, the impact of government policy—such as import substitution—on the rate of diffusion of computer technology is analyzed. Third, the influence of politics on the international diffusion of television broadcasting is discussed.

In the conclusion, the analyses of the workforce structure (Part I) and technological trends (Part II) in developing countries are viewed jointly in the context of the overall argument. Based on these findings, we explore the policy and strategic implications for the future of the information sector in developing countries.

## NOTES

1. Information occupations comprise activities such as industrial management, government administration, clerical work, banking, education, and research (Porat 1975; Jonscher 1983). Information technologies are defined as all mechanical or electronic devices—as well as a standard set of procedures—that increase the natural human capability of transmitting, storing, and processing information (Jonscher 1983; Keen and Scott Morton 1978).

2. In particular, see Machlup (1962); Bell (1973); Porat (1975); OECD (1981); Barnes and Lamberton (1976); Wall (1977); and Pool et al. (1984).

3. According to Bell (1979), the term "information society" defines those societies where the dominant labor activity is information processing, rather than industrial or agricultural production ("a society can be characterized by what most of its people do"). Thus, the reference to information societies in the developing world would contradict Bell's definition.

While it is true that there are few developing countries in which information processing is the dominant labor activity, it is also true that most nations—including the less developed—contain "pockets" of information societies, generaly located around the political and economic centers.

4. Jussawalla and Chee-Wah-Cheah (1982) and Vitro (1984) are among the few researchers who have conducted country studies of the information sector in developing nations.

5. See Bell (1973).

6. See Sabolo, Gaude, and Wery (1975); Blades, Johnston, and Marcezewski (1974); Katouzian (1970); Bhalla (1973); Gemmel (1982); and Singelmann (1978).

7. This notion, "dysfunctional education system" in developing countries, is discussed later in greater detail in Chapter 2.

8. This is particularly true for countries at lower levels of development.

9. The scholars who studied communications and political development (Pye 1963; Lerner 1958) explored political participation as a variable, but did not consider state-building processes. In the case of developed countries, recent research trends seem to turn away from political explanatory variables, and focus on economic factors. This statement should not be extended to the neo-Marxist literature—which has been rich in formulating hypotheses, but poor in supplying evidence as to the real interaction between political structures and communications.

It should be mentioned, though, that utilization of the political variable in explaining international diffusion of technologies can be found in fields other than that of communications (see De Leon 1979; Price 1965).

10. See Deutsch (1957; 1963; 1964; 1967).

11. See Bell (1973); Porat (1977); and Jonscher (1983).

# PART I

# THE INFORMATION WORKFORCE IN DEVELOPING COUNTRIES

Part I focuses on the analysis of changes in the information workforce. It has three objectives: (1) to describe the changes in the sectoral and occupational structure of employment that have taken place in developing countries, with special emphasis on the growth of the information sector; (2) to compare the process of the occupational transformation in developing countries with that of industrialized nations; and (3) to analyze the relationship between the growth of the information sector, economic development, and expansion of governments.

Chapter 1 presents comparative data on the size and internal structure of the information workforce in developed and developing countries. While data presented shows that there is a worldwide growth of information occupations, it also supports the notion that growth patterns differ widely according to each country.

Chapter 2 then identifies the factors that determine the divergent development patterns of the information workforce. Data presented in Chapter 2 supports the hypothesis that the growth of the information sector in developing countries is driven primarily by the growth of the government sector, and the role played by the state absorbing the surplus of educated labor that cannot be employed in the private sector. At higher levels of development, industrialization starts driving the need for information workers to manage increasingly complex production processes. At this point, industrialization and economic growth become the main variable driving information sector growth.

# 1

## Measurement and Cross-National Comparisons of the Information Workforce

The research literature of the past ten years has provided substantial evidence showing that, in the course of economic development, there is a shift in the occupational composition of employment within each industrial sector (i.e., agriculture, manufacturing, and services), increasing their respective portions of information occupations—leading to the emergence of a sizable information-intensive sector. Causes for this shift range from the substitution of information for noninformation labor in the manufacturing sector, to changes in the internal composition of the service sector (away from personal services to social and distributive services). This chapter analyzes the worldwide emergence of an information sector in the workforce structure, and highlights this change in developing countries.

Cross-sectional time series for selected countries show the lack of commonality of the development pattern leading to the emergence of an information sector. Indeed, data indicates that countries follow different patterns of sectoral transformation of their labor force, depending on: (1) the time at which they start to industrialize; (2) the internal economic and political conditions; and (3) the country's position within the system of international trade.

To present our evidence, we first discuss the concept of information worker as defined in the scholarly literature. Second, we draw on the extensive data generated to-date in developed countries. Third, we analyze comparative data on the size of the information workforce in selected developing countries, and assess development paths.

An earlier version of this chapter was published in *The Information Society* 4 (December 1986).

## GROWTH OF INFORMATION OCCUPATIONS
## AS A KEY FEATURE OF INFORMATION SOCIETIES

The empirical analysis of the sectoral composition of the labor force has been utilized ever since Simon Kusnetz (1957) tested different hypotheses with regard to changes in the economic structure of countries undergoing industrialization. Based on the pioneering work of Fisher (1933) and Clark (1957), Simon Kusnetz divided the workforces of a number of nations into the primary sector (principally extractive), the secondary sector (primarily manufacturing), and the tertiary sector (services). He defined the service sector as composed of those workers employed in trade, finance, real estate, transport and communications, personal service, business, domestic service, the professions, and government. In a later work, Kusnetz expressed concern about the lack of information on this sector:

Despite the magnitude of the service sector, the measurement of its output is mostly subject to error, and data and knowledge are far too scanty to permit adequate analysis. It may seem ironic that we know less about this sector which includes groups engaged in the production and spread of basic and applied knowledge, as well as those concerned with major political and social decisions, than about the other sectors; but it is not surprising, for activities that are not within the repetitive patterns of large-scale operation are for that reason not readily subject to measurement or analysis. (Kusnetz 1966, 143–44)

In the early 1960s, several leading economists started isolating a fourth occupational sector of the workforce, defined as knowledge intensive or information based. However, it took more than 15 years for scholars to agree on a more or less stable definition of the information worker. Throughout the 1960s and 1970s, the concept of information-intensive occupations was defined in various ways, depending on which theoretical construct supported data-gathering efforts aimed at measuring the information sector.

In the first attempt to measure the share of knowledge-based occupations in the U.S. workforce, Fritz Machlup (1962) defined the knowledge industry as consisting of education, research, publishing, and broadcasting. He estimated that 31 percent of the total workforce in the United States was employed in the knowledge industry in 1958.

Eleven years later, Bell (1973) also attempted to measure the share of knowledge workers in the U.S. workforce. However, Bell employed a much stricter definition of knowledge worker, including only information producers and excluding information transmitters. The difference in the two approaches is substantial. In Bell's terms, "the chief census category [he is] concerned with is that of professional and technical persons" (1973, 214). This category includes teachers, engineers, engineering and service technicians, and scientists.

The main reason for the difference in Bell's and Machlup's definitions of the knowledge industry worker is one of intent. Fritz Machlup's (1962) objective was to compute the proportion of the U.S. workforce engaged in the production and distribution of knowledge. For that purpose, he grouped 30 industries into five major classes of knowledge production, processing, and distribution: (1) education, (2) research and development, (3) media of communication, (4) information machines, and (5) information services.

Bell considered Machlup's definition to be too broad and all inclusive:

Any meaningful figure about the "knowledge society" would be much smaller. The calculation would have to be restricted largely to research, higher education, and the production of knowledge, as I have defined it, or as intellectual property, which involves valid new knowledge and its disseminations. (Bell 1973, 212-13)

As a result of these two different definitions of the knowledge society, the size of knowledge occupations varied widely in both studies. Contrary to Machlup's 31 percent, Bell (1973) estimated that, in 1963, the professional and technical occupations—the core of the "knowledge society"—represented 12.2 percent of the total civilian employment.

The concept of "information" society—developed in the mid-1970s—was slightly different from that of the "knowledge" society. The research body initiated by Marc Porat (1975) defined information workers as those engaged in creating or processing information. Porat's initial question was, "How large is the segment of the workforce which primarily produces, processes, or distributes information, goods and services and how is that workforce distributed among industries?" (1975, 4). In order to respond to this question, Porat defined three subsectors of the information workforce:

| | |
|---|---|
| Subsector A: | Workers whose final product is information |
| Subsector B: | Workers whose main activity is informational in nature |
| | – Information creators ("knowledge workers") |
| | – Information transmittors |
| | – Information processors |
| Subsector C: | Workers who operate information technologies |

Porat's classification differed from Machlup's in many respects. The greatest difference resided in the broadness of Machlup's categories. He included a variety of activities not considered by Porat. For example, religious activities and education in the armed forces were considered informational and educational (M.I.T. 1982). Communications media included all commercial printing, stationery, and office supplies. Information machines included musical instruments, signaling devices, and typewriters. Information services included securities brokers and real estate agents.

Yes, despite these differences, Porat was closer to Machlup than to Bell. By including workers whose final product is information or communication (Subsector A), and workers who make, service, and repair information technologies, Porat was focusing on the production *and* distribution of knowledge, whereas

Bell had focused only on the production of knowledge. For Bell, the essence of the shifting base of the U.S. economy from agricultural to postindustrial resided in the increasing production of information, knowledge, and ideas—as distinct from manufactured goods. For Porat, production of information could not be separated from its delivery and usage.

The difference between Machlup and Porat resides in Porat's inclusion in the information category of workers who use information. For Machlup, the knowledge sector included those workers engaged in the production and distribution of knowledge. Porat's information sector included not only workers producing and distributing knowledge, but also those utilizing information as a productive input, "regardless of the industrial branches to which their jobs belong" (Uno 1982, 148).[1] Porat's all-encompassing definition is the one that has been generally adopted for describing the information sector of the labor force. In a later work prepared for the Department of Commerce, Porat (1977) further refined his classification of information workers. Of the 422 occupations used by the U.S. Bureau of Labor Statistics for compiling data on occupations by industry, 188 were identified by Porat as information workers. These were classified in five functional categories, which corresponded to the subsectors that had originally been defined by Porat in 1975:

1. Knowledge producers
2. Knowledge distributors
3. Market search and coordination specialists
4. Information processors
5. Information machine workers

Using this framework and extracting data from occupational censuses, Porat concluded that—by 1960—the predominant occupational sector in the United States was informational in nature, and estimated that—by 1980—workers who either produced information as a final product or used information as an intermediate product would constitute around half of the U.S. workforce.

Porat's work started a series of research efforts in different countries aimed at identifying a possible common trend in industrialized economies toward the development of a sizable information sector. In 1976, Barnes and Lamberton analyzed the Australian workforce according to Porat's classification—using census data from 1911 to 1971. The authors determined that 25.5 percent of the total Australian workforce in 1971 was engaged in information occupations. A year later, Wall (1977) showed that, in 1971, 36.6 percent of Britain's economically active population was engaged in information processing and information-related employment. In the same year, Lange and Rempp (1977) determined that 30.7 percent of the total West German workforce was classified as being predominantly information related.

In 1980, the Expert Group of the OECD's Information, Computer, and Communications Working Party started a project aimed (among other things) at measuring the size of the information workforce in several industrialized countries. The typology of information occupations devised by the Expert Group (OECD 1981) used a four-subsector classification, which aggregated Porat's sectors (1) and (3) into a single group:

- Information producers
- Information processors
- Information distributors
- Information infrastructure occupations

Since the raw data to be used by the OECD were obtained from national statistics that utilized the 1968 International Standard Classification of Occupations (ISCO), the study defined an inventory of "information occupations" with their associated ISCO two-digit code numbers.[2]

The inventory devised by the OECD constitutes a most useful tool for performing detailed comparative analysis of the information workforce at the country level. The particular advantage of the OECD project is that the measurement of the information sector in several countries was based on a common set of principles for defining information activities and procedures—which had been prepared in advance by the organization's secretariat. Two years later, Vitro (1984) used the OECD typology for performing an analysis of the Venezuelan information sector.

Instead of utilizing the OECD inventory of information occupations, other authors attempted a direct aggregation of workers—such as Porat did in the mid-1970s. For example, Jonscher (1982b) defined a study-specific classification of information occupations, which matched—more or less closely—that of the OECD and Porat. However, Jonscher's definition of the information sector of the U.S. economy seemed to be larger than Porat's. He estimated that, in 1980, the information workforce would account for 47,205,000 workers (Porat estimated 44,650,721).

Other authors have considered definitions that are still more restrictive than those of Porat and the OECD. For example, Uno (1982) defined knowledge workers as only those who utilize knowledge as an input for production. Thus, by knowledge workers, he referred to the following:

- Natural science specialists, including scientific researchers, engineers, and technicians;
- Social science specialists, including judicial workers and registered accountants;
- Educators, including professors and teachers;
- Medical specialists;
- Artists, including authors, reporters, editors, fine artists, designers, and photographers;
- Managers, including government officials, directors of companies and corporations, and other managers and administrators; and
- Clerical workers.

According to the study performed by Uno on the Japanese workforce, knowledge workers as a percentage of the total workforce increased from 7.3 percent in 1960 to 11.5 percent in 1975.

Despite the multiple approaches utilized to measure the information sector, most scholars' views seem to be coinciding with Porat's comprehensive definition of information occupations—as portrayed by the OECD which includes not only the producers of information, but also its distributors and final users in the production process (see Table 1.1). The main conclusion to be drawn from these studies is that despite the differences in the definition of the information sector, all authors have consistently shown an increase in information-based occupations as a share of the total employment in any given country.

**Table 1.1**
**Definitions Used in Studies of the Information Workforce**

| COUNTRY STUDIED | STUDY | YEAR | SECTOR DEFINITION | TYPOLOGY USED |
|---|---|---|---|---|
| United States | Machlup (1962) | 1958 | Knowledge-based Industries | Study-specific |
| | Bell (1973) | 1963 | Knowledge Occupations | Study-specific |
| | Porat (1976) | 1860-1970 | Information Sector | Porat |
| | Jonscher (1982a) | 1900-1970 | Information Occupations | Study-specific |
| | OECD (1981) | 1950-1970 | Information Sector | OECD |
| Australia | Barnes and Lamberton (1976) | 1911-1971 | Information Sector | Porat |
| United Kingdom | Wall (1977) | 1841-1971 | Information Sector | Porat OECD |
| | OECD (1981) | 1951-1971 | Information Labor Force | |
| West Germany | Lange and Rempp (1977) | 1950-1971 | Information Sector | Porat |
| | OECD (1981) | 1951-1978 | Information Labor Force | OECD |
| Canada | OECD (1981) | 1951-1971 | Information Sector | OECD |
| Finland | OECD (1981) | 1970-1975 | Information Sector | OECD |
| France | OECD (1981) | 1954-1975 | Information Sector | OECD |
| Sweden | OECD (1981) | 1960-1975 | Information Sector | OECD |
| Austria | OECD (1981) | 1951-1971 | Information Sector | OECD |
| Japan | OECD (1981) | 1960-1975 | Knowledge Occupations | OECD |
| | Uno (1982) | 1960-1975 | Information Sector | Study-specific |
| Venezuela | Vitro (1984) | 1978 | | OECD |

*Source:* Compiled by the author.

However, the measurement of the information workforce over time raised two methodological issues. First, is it possible to compare the size of the information sector for a given country in 1860 and 1980? This issue was originally raised by Lamberton:

Even a cursory glance at the list of information occupations included in the information sector reveals that many of those occupations have made their appearance in the list in the last few decades. (Lamberton 1982, 41)

Lamberton considered that any comparative study based on time-series statistics should differentiate between expansion of the information sector due to economic growth and increase in demand for information occupations caused by incremental division of labor and specialization.

Second, cross-national comparisons raise the issue of external validity (Webb and Campbell 1973). Information sectors in two countries might differ greatly in their internal structure and characteristics. For example, two countries may have the same proportion of their labor force employed in information-related occupations; but one country might have a concentration in government staff, and the second country might feature a strong private business sector.[3] Can we still talk of an undifferentiated growth of the information workforce? Or in each country, must we confine ourselves to the category of the specific areas of growth, such as "white collarization" or "bureaucratic expansion"? To avoid the latter dead-end, cross-national research has to deal with this issue by providing disaggregated data that is susceptible to in-depth comparisons of processes of different nature.[4]

Therefore, the scholarly work done to date on the concept of information worker provides a firm definitional basis for our own study. However, as shown in Table 1.1, all workforce studies—with one exception—have been performed on developed economies. As a result, there is a serious lack of evidence with regard to the occurrence of this social phenomenon in developing countries. We shall lay the basis for our evidence on the latter by first applying our arguments to those countries for which the most data is currently available: the developed countries.

## EMERGENCE OF AN INFORMATION WORKFORCE: IS THERE A DISTINCTIVE PATH IN DEVELOPED COUNTRIES?

The figures set out in Table 1.2 summarize the long-term trend in the breakdown of the labor force of four developed countries. Data were compiled from different national studies. As a consequence, complete agreement as to the precise inventory of occupations to be designated "information intensive" is unlikely. It should be pointed out, though, that changes in classification could yield results that diverge in magnitude, rather than trend.

**Table 1.2**
**Transformations in the Workforce Structure of Four Developed Countries**

| | 1840 | 1850 | 1860 | 1870 | 1880 | 1890 | 1900 | 1910 | 1920 | 1930 | 1940 | 1950 | 1960 | 1970 | 1980 |
|---|---|---|---|---|---|---|---|---|---|---|---|---|---|---|---|
| *Agriculture* | | | | | | | | | | | | | | | |
| United Kingdom | 21.6 | 21.0 | 20.3 | 16.2 | 12.1 | 10.2 | 8.2 | 7.6 | 7.3 | 6.4 | 5.8 | 5.2 | 3.9 | 3.0 | |
| United States | | | 40.6 | 47.0 | 43.7 | 37.2 | 35.3 | 31.1 | 32.5 | 20.4 | 15.4 | 11.9 | 6.0 | 3.1 | 2.1 |
| Australia | | | | | | | | 31.0 | 27.0 | 23.2 | 19.9 | 16.5 | 12.0 | 9.1 | 7.4 |
| Germany | | | | | | | | | | | | 22.5 | | | 5.8 |
| *Industry* | | | | | | | | | | | | | | | |
| United Kingdom | 44.0 | 45.6 | 47.2 | 48.4 | 49.5 | 47.5 | 45.4 | 43.4 | 43.2 | 45.2 | 42.6 | 39.9 | 36.1 | 33.7 | |
| United States | | 37.0 | 32.0 | 25.2 | 28.1 | 26.8 | 36.3 | 32.0 | 35.3 | 37.2 | 38.3 | 34.8 | 28.6 | 22.5 | |
| Australia | | | | | | | | 27.0 | 27.5 | 30.9 | 32.0 | 33.0 | 33.0 | 31.2 | 26.7 |
| Germany | | | | | | | | | | | | 38.3 | | | 35.1 |
| *Services* | | | | | | | | | | | | | | | |
| United Kingdom | 29.8 | 28.4 | 26.9 | 28.7 | 30.5 | 32.3 | 34.0 | 35.7 | 29.7 | 27.5 | 27.3 | 27.1 | 26.9 | 26.7 | |
| United States | | 16.6 | 16.2 | 24.6 | 22.3 | 25.1 | 17.7 | 17.8 | 19.8 | 22.5 | 19.0 | 17.2 | 21.9 | 28.8 | |
| Australia | | | | | | | | 33.5 | 34.0 | 30.3 | 32.7 | 35.0 | 32.5 | 32.2 | 35.6 |
| Germany | | | | | | | | | | | | 20.9 | | | 25.9 |
| *Information* | | | | | | | | | | | | | | | |
| United Kingdom | 4.6 | 5.1 | 5.6 | 6.8 | 7.9 | 10.2 | 12.4 | 13.3 | 19.8 | 20.9 | 24.4 | 27.8 | 33.1 | 36.6 | |
| United States | | 5.8 | 4.8 | 6.5 | 12.4 | 12.8 | 14.9 | 17.7 | 24.5 | 24.9 | 30.8 | 42.0 | 46.4 | 46.6 | |
| Australia | | | | | | | | 8.5 | 11.5 | 15.6 | 16.3 | 17.0 | 22.5 | 27.5 | 30.2 |
| Germany | | | | | | | | | | | | 18.3 | 24.6 | 30.7 | 33.2 |

*Sources:* Bell (1979); Wall (1977); Lamberton (1982); and Lange and Rempp (1977).

As for the problem of intercountry comparison of independently derived data, Pool et al.—comparing information flows in the United States and Japan—argued that differences in trends and rates can be trusted much more than absolute differences in figures for levels of flow:

In this respect the situation for our communications indices resembles that for other social indicators such as unemployment rates. Anyone who works with such statistics knows that unemployment is defined differently in different countries. In the absence of other knowledge, finding that the unemployment index in country A is 7% and in country B, 6%, would hardly justify saying that there is more unemployment in country A. It could be the other way around.

On the other hand, if each keeps its national statistics consistently, over time, a change in the index within a country is probably meaningful. If unemployment, as defined and measured in country A, rises by 10%, and by 5%, as defined and measured in country B, we are probably justified in concluding that the difference is real. It is still hypothetically possible, although improbable, that the difference in rate of change was entirely within those categories in which the definition differed. (Pool et al. 1984)[5]

The same point applies to the comparison of workforce structures in different countries.

Several common trends can be identified in Table 1.2: (1) The proportion of the labor force in the agricultural sector has been declining in all countries, at least since the late 1800s; (2) a similar trend—albeit at a more moderate pace—can be identified in the industrial sector; (3) the service sector remains an aggregate of growing industries, except in the United Kingdom; and (4) the information sector has been growing at a rapid pace in all four countries.

Even before entering the phase of modern industrialization that started after World World I, the four countries under consideration had already commenced the process of absorption of the agricultural labor force. In the case of the United Kingdom, this process started in the eighteenth century; in the case of the United States, in the mid-1800s; and in Australia, at the end of the nineteenth century.

In parallel to this decrease in the size of the agricultural sector, all three countries experienced an increase of the industrial sector. This trend confirms Colin Clark's analysis for developed countries referred to in the first section (Clark 1957). Consistent with the Clark-Fisher theory, the share of labor employed in services increased between 1900 and 1950 in all four countries. This trend continued until 1970/1980—except for the United Kingdom, where a decline is observed.

The expansion of the information sector that can be observed in all four countries is a phenomenon identifiable throughout the developed world. Figure 1.1 presents the changes of the workforce structure in four developed countries (United States, United Kingdom, Germany, and Australia).

As shown in Figure 1.1, the information has been expanding in all industrialized countries, albeit at varying growth rates. Two growth patterns can be identified. In the United States and the United Kingdom, the growth of the information sector was clearly in full force before the turn of the century, while in other developed countries such as Australia and Germany, growth was delayed until mid-1900 as a result of specific country developments.

In the first case of the United States and the United Kingdom, the emergence of an information sector began at a much earlier point in time, approximately the late 1800s. Growth rates for both countries evolve almost in parallel until the mid-1900s, when the United States continued its process of information sector expansion, while the share of information workers in Britain stagnated. A brief review of each country reveals the reasons for similarity and then divergence.

In the U.S., it is remarkable to see how closely the expansion of the information sector (Figure 1.1a) follows the process of industrialization. Industrialization started in the United States in the first half of the nineteenth century. By the mid-1800s, manufacturing industries expanded significantly, thereby indicating the forthcoming shift from an agricultural economy to an industrial economy. Between 1860 and 1870, industrial growth slowed down because of the Civil War. The agricultural sector in the United States expanded—while the industrial, services, and information sectors stagnated.

Shortly after the Civil War, the economy recovered very quickly and grew at a very fast pace. As shown in Figure 1.1a, after 1870—and especially after 1880—the information, industrial, and service sectors grew—while agriculture declined. Indeed, associated with the rapid growth of the economy in the postwar period were the emergence of a national banking system and the expansion of services that fostered, in turn, the growth of the information sector. In fact,

**Figure 1.1**
**Structure of the Workforce in Developed Countries (Four-Sector Aggregation)**

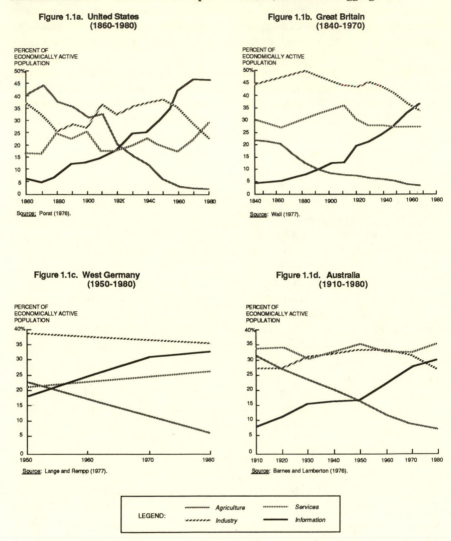

Figure 1.1a. United States
(1860-1980)

Figure 1.1b. Great Britain
(1840-1970)

Figure 1.1c. West Germany
(1950-1980)

Figure 1.1d. Australia
(1910-1980)

Source: Porat (1976).

Source: Wall (1977).

Source: Lange and Rempp (1977).

Source: Barnes and Lamberton (1976).

LEGEND:  —————— Agriculture   ············ Services
         -------- Industry      ———— Information

the most dramatic gains in employment between 1910 and 1920 occurred in transportation, trade, and finance (Singelmann 1978).

By the end of the 1920s, economic growth again came to a halt; and with it, the expansion of the information sector. However, the recovery after World War II resulted in a renewed expansion. Since 1960, a new phenomenon in the growth pattern of the sector has occurred. In the past 150 years, sector contractions occurred as a result of either war (1860) or economic depression (1930), and were momentary. The year 1960 marks the peak in the growth of the information sector, after which—despite the overall economic expansion—it has remained at a stable level. According to Jonscher, this stabilization is due to structural factors:

Information worker productivity will grow faster than that of production workers. This will result in a levelling off and then a decline in the proportion of information workers in the economy, the ratio reaching almost exactly 50% at the peak. By 1990 the percentage of information workers will have fallen to about 49%; by the end of the century it is forecast... to have dropped to under 46%. (Jonscher 1983, 25)[6]

Thus, in the United States, the expansion of the information sector was economic in nature, following closely the process of industrialization. However, the correlation between the growth of the information workforce and the process of industrialization is not as clear in the British example (see Figure 1.1b). In the United States, the expansion of both industrial and information sectors occurred in parallel, at least between 1880 and 1940; but in Great Britain, the industrial workforce had achieved a share of more than 40 percent of the labor force before the information sector started to grow.

This difference between growth patterns has to do with distinct industrialization paths. Industrialization in Britain was achieved a century and a half before the United States started its own. In addition—contrary to what happened in the United States—when 44 percent of the British labor force was engaged in industry, less than 5 percent was dedicated to information-related tasks. Interestingly enough, Britain seems to have reached the "apogee of its economic leadership and influence between 1850 and 1870" (Kindleberger 1969, 29), at a relative low level of expansion of its information sector.

The British pattern would seem to counter—in principle—the universal and structural trend pointed out by Jonscher (1983), which stated that the tendency toward an increase in specialization in the production process (which, in turn, leads to an expansion of the information sector) is part of the industrialization process (see Chapter 2). In fact, one could argue that specialization is not so much an irreversible trend as it is a management style consciously adopted by managers in the manufacturing sector.

Furthermore, we could hypothesize that the British economy's relative decline during the second half of the nineteenth century is partly due to the lack of expansion of the information sector, resulting in productive inefficiencies. This argument would seem to be confirmed by the proposition set forth by a British economist:

She [Britain] was too deeply committed to the technology and business organization of the first phase of industrialization, which had served her so well, to advance enthusiastically into the field of the new revolutionary technology and industrial management which came to the fore in the 1890s. (Hobsbawn 1969, 131)

As a result, during the twentieth century, the development of the British information sector followed a pattern slightly different from that evidenced in the U.S. Starting in 1890, the growth of the information sector was the result of sectoral shifts from industry and services to information occupations. By 1900, the United Kingdom was well beyond the second phase of Colin Clark's model; and, therefore, no further transfer would occur from agriculture to other sectors. In addition to this difference, no evidence is found—at least until 1970—of a slowing of the information sector's growth rate, as was the case in the U.S.

However, in contrast to the nineteenth-century beginnings of an information sector in the U.S. and the U.K., other industrialized countries show later development in sync with their respective histories. For Germany, statistics (Figure 1.1c) show that the growth of the information sector occurred largely between 1950 and 1980, driven by reconstruction as the country redeveloped an efficient industrial base capable of competing in international markets. The growth of the information sector was the result of a shift in the labor force from agricultural to service and information occupations. The decrease in the share of industrial occupations is not highly significant when compared to the recent trends in the United States and the United Kingdom.

The evolution of the Australian workforce (Figure 1.1d) shows yet another profile. Between 1910 and 1960, a simultaneous growth of the industrial and information sectors can be observed. The expansion of both sectors—combined with the stagnation of the service occupations—led to a fast decrease of the agricultural sector, which changed from a 31 percent share in 1910 to 7.4 percent in 1980.

A brief overview of the evolution of the workforce structure of four industrialized nations has shown that, although the expansion of the information

**Table 1.3**
**Percentage Point Change in Information Workforce Share**

|                | 1960 – 1970 | 1970 – 1975 |
|----------------|:-----------:|:-----------:|
| United States  | 4.4         | 0.1         |
| United Kingdom | 3.5         | —           |
| Australia      | 5.0         | 1.4         |
| Germany        | 5.9         | 2.0         |
| Japan          | 7.5         | 4.2         |
| France         | 4.4         | 3.6         |
| Canada         | 5.7         | —           |
| Sweden         | 6.6         | 2.3         |

*Source:* Compiled by the author from OECD (1981).

sector is a universal phenomenon, its development patterns vary substantially across countries. Moreover, if we compare growth ratios of the information sector for a larger sample of countries, we see significant variances in growth (see Table 1.3).

The United States and the United Kingdom, which started their industrialization at an earlier stage than the other countries, seem to be reaching a peak in the expansion of their information sectors. The other countries are still experiencing information sector growth at faster rates. Particularly interesting is the case of Japan, which exhibits unusually high growth rates. However, for the developed countries there is a large similarity in the direction of growth for their economies' principal sectors—agriculture, industry, services and information. Table 1.4 shows the current status of sector changes in developed countries. With the exception of Japan and France, Table 1.4 reveals a remarkable consistency among developed countries. In all other developed countries, the service and information sectors are growing, while the agricultural and industrial sectors are declining. In other words, we are in the midst of a global trend resulting from the combination of declining agricultural and industrial occupations with expanding service and information occupations.

In light of this global pattern, we can conclude that, even though each country exhibits specific sectoral patterns of development, there seems to be a converging trend toward a unifying path shared by all industrialized nations. It is appropriate now to study the changes occurring in developing countries, in order to assert the applicability of this conclusion to the Third World.

**Table 1.4**
**Current Status in Sectoral Changes in Industrialized Countries**

|  | GROWS | STAGNATES | DECLINES |
|---|---|---|---|
| AGRICULTURE |  |  | U.K.., U.S., Australia, France, Japan, Sweden, Germany, U.K. |
| INDUSTRY | Japan | France | U.S., Australia, Sweden, Germany, U.K. |
| SERVICES | Australia, U.S., France, Japan, Sweden, Germany |  |  |
| INFORMATION | Australia, U.S., France, Japan, Sweden, Germany, U.K. |  |  |

*Source:* Compiled by the author.

## MEASURING THE INFORMATION WORKFORCE
## IN DEVELOPING COUNTRIES

As stated, measurement of the size and growth of the information workforce in developing countries is surprisingly scarce. A comprehensive search of the field at the time of the study only surfaced two research studies, both country cases.[7]

Vitro (1984) prepared a report on the Venezuelan information sector—using the OECD methodology to measure both the share of the information workforce in the total population and the contribution of the information sector to the gross domestic product (GDP). He concluded that, in 1978, 26.3 percent of the economically active individuals should be considered as information workers. In addition, the information sector constituted between 20 percent and 25 percent of the gross domestic product in the same year. Despite the fact that he does not supply comparative figures for other years, Vitro (1984) argues that the Venezuelan economy is undergoing a profound structural change, from "an economy based on a non-renewable energy source—petroleum— . . . to an economy based on a renewable energy resource [information]" (p. 8).

Jussawalla and Chee-Wah-Cheah (1982) measured the size of the information sector in Singapore—using an input-output framework, where industries

**Table 1.5**
**Four-Sector Aggregation of the Workforce Structure**
**in the Developing World (in percent)**

| | Agriculture | | | Industry | | | Services | | | Information | | |
|---|---|---|---|---|---|---|---|---|---|---|---|---|
| | C. 1960 | C. 1970 | C. 1980 | C. 1960 | C. 1970 | C. 1980 | C.1960 | C.1970 | C. 1980 | C. 1960 | C. 1970 | C.1980 |
| Argentina | 19.5 | 15.4 | 16.2 | 33.9 | 32.3 | 26.8 | 25.3 | 30.5 | 32.9 | 21.2 | 21.8 | 24.1 |
| Bahrain | - - - | 7.1 | 3.7 | - - - | 47.1 | 43.6 | - - - | 27.1 | 26.4 | - - - | 18.6 | 26.3 |
| Brazil | 55.8 | 46.0 | - - - | 15.9 | 17.4 | - - - | 16.2 | 24.5 | - - - | 12.0 | 12.2 | - - - |
| Chile | 29.3 | 22.7 | 16.8 | 30.8 | 31.7 | 31.1 | 25.3 | 25.6 | 29.7 | 14.6 | 20.0 | 22.3 |
| Egypt | 54.7 | 51.4 | 40.7 | 16.5 | 18.5 | 21.4 | 20.8 | 17.6 | 19.2 | 8.0 | 12.4 | 18.6 |
| Ghana | 61.1 | 57.4 | - - - | 16.7 | 17.5 | - - - | 17.7 | 18.2 | - - - | 4.6 | 6.9 | - - - |
| Hong Kong | 7.1 | 4.0 | 1.5 | 44.4 | 48.9 | 46.0 | 34.3 | 31.3 | 29.0 | 14.2 | 15.8 | 23.5 |
| India | 73.1 | 72.4 | 69.3 | 14.9 | 12.6 | 14.4 | 7.6 | 8.4 | 8.7 | 4.4 | 6.6 | 7.6 |
| Iran | 75.0 | 48.6 | - - - | 13.4 | 28.8 | - - - | 8.0 | 14.7 | - - - | 3.6 | 7.9 | - - - |
| Korea | 66.2 | 51.1 | 34.0 | 10.1 | 20.1 | 26.0 | 17.4 | 18.7 | 25.4 | 6.3 | 10.1 | 14.6 |
| Kuwait | - - - | 1.6 | 2.0 | - - - | 41.1 | 38.0 | - - - | 33.6 | 30.1 | - - - | 23.7 | 29.9 |
| Mexico | 53.5 | 40.3 | 31.5 | 19.9 | 22.5 | 27.4 | 16.0 | 20.6 | 20.1 | 10.6 | 16.5 | 20.9 |
| Pakistan | 76.0 | 58.0 | 54.8 | 11.0 | 18.5 | 20.7 | 9.3 | 18.8 | 18.1 | 3.7 | 4.7 | 6.4 |
| Panama | 50.7 | 38.8 | 28.1 | 14.0 | 17.8 | 19.1 | 21.5 | 26.8 | 26.4 | 13.7 | 16.6 | 26.4 |
| Philippines | 66.1 | 54.9 | 52.1 | 13.5 | 15.2 | 15.2 | 14.6 | 19.4 | 22.0 | 5.8 | 10.5 | 10.8 |
| Singapore | 7.9 | 4.3 | 1.9 | 31.4 | 32.1 | 32.6 | 43.6 | 39.4 | 35.5 | 17.1 | 24.1 | 30.0 |
| Sri Lanka | 52.2 | 50.1 | 45.3 | 20.2 | 22.4 | 25.2 | 18.3 | 16.8 | 17.7 | 9.3 | 10.6 | 11.8 |
| Syria | 52.7 | 50.9 | 32.2 | 23.6 | 24.6 | 33.4 | 17.3 | 15.5 | 16.9 | 6.3 | 8.9 | 17.6 |
| Tunisia | - - - | 39.1 | 33.9 | - - - | 36.1 | 38.7 | - - - | 14.8 | 15.3 | - - - | 10.0 | 12.1 |
| Venezuela | 34.1 | 23.4 | 14.5 | 21.4 | 23.5 | 25.0 | 30.4 | 31.9 | 34.9 | 14.1 | 21.3 | 25.6 |

LEGEND: - - - *Data Not Available*

*Source:* Katz (1986a). Based on ILO statistics (see Appendix A).

were either classified as totally or partially information intensive. Using Singapore's input-output table for 1973, the authors established that, as a whole, the information sector comprised 24 percent of the nation's GDP. This figure was considered by the authors as an indicator of structural changes in an economy that "is increasingly being redirected from an export-oriented manufacturing base to one based on the export of services" (Jussawalla and Chee-Wah-Cheah 1982, 11).

Significantly, both works consider the expansion of the information sector in the developing world as a phenomenon similar to that occurring in developed countries, where information sector growth is driven by industrialization. In order to test the general validity of Vitro's and Jussawalla's conclusions for all developing countries, data measuring the size of the information sector was generated through the methodology described in Appendix A. Table 1.5 presents summary statistics on changes in the four sectors in 20 developing countries between 1960 and 1980. For the same sectors and countries, Table 1.6 shows the average percentage change in occupational shares for the period. Standard deviations are given as one indicator of the degree of similarity of sector share changes across countries (Gemmel 1982).[8]

Data shows that the share of industrial, service, and information occupations tends to increase; and the agricultural share consistently falls. Significantly, the

**Table 1.6**
**Change in Sectoral Share of the Workforce in the Developing World (in percent)**

| | Agriculture | | Industry | | Services | | Information | |
|---|---|---|---|---|---|---|---|---|
| | 1960–70 | 1970–80 | 1960–70 | 1970–80 | 1960–70 | 1970–80 | 1960–70 | 1970–80 |
| Argentina | −4.1 | 0.8 | −1.6 | −5.5 | 5.2 | 2.4 | 0.6 | 2.3 |
| Bahrain | | −3.4 | | −3.5 | | −0.7 | | 7.7 |
| Brazil | −9.8 | | 1.5 | | 8.3 | | 0.2 | |
| Chile | −6.6 | −5.9 | 0.9 | −0.6 | 0.3 | 4.1 | 5.4 | 2.3 |
| Egypt | −3.3 | −10.7 | 2.0 | 2.9 | −3.2 | 1.6 | 4.4 | 6.2 |
| Ghana | −3.7 | | 0.8 | | 0.5 | | 2.3 | |
| Hong Kong | −3.1 | −2.5 | 4.5 | −2.9 | −3.0 | −2.3 | 1.6 | 7.7 |
| India | −0.7 | −3.1 | −2.3 | 1.8 | 0.8 | 0.3 | 2.2 | 1.0 |
| Iran | −26.4 | | 15.4 | | 6.7 | | 4.3 | |
| Korea | −15.1 | −17.1 | 10.0 | 5.9 | 1.3 | 6.7 | 3.8 | 4.5 |
| Kuwait | | 0.4 | | −3.1 | | −3.5 | | 6.2 |
| Mexico | −13.2 | −8.8 | 2.6 | 4.9 | 4.6 | −0.5 | 5.9 | 4.4 |
| Pakistan | −18.0 | −3.2 | 7.5 | 2.2 | 9.5 | −0.7 | 1.0 | 1.7 |
| Panama | −11.9 | −10.7 | 3.8 | 1.3 | 5.3 | −0.4 | 2.9 | 9.8 |
| Philippines | −11.2 | −2.8 | 1.7 | 0.0 | 4.8 | 2.6 | 4.7 | 0.3 |
| Singapore | −3.6 | −2.4 | 0.7 | 0.5 | −4.2 | −3.9 | 7.0 | 5.9 |
| Sri Lanka | −2.1 | −4.8 | 2.2 | 2.8 | −1.5 | 0.9 | 1.3 | 1.2 |
| Syria | −1.8 | −18.7 | 1.0 | 8.8 | −1.8 | 1.4 | 2.6 | 8.7 |
| Tunisia | | −5.2 | | 2.6 | | 0.5 | | 2.1 |
| Venezuela | −10.7 | −8.9 | 2.1 | 1.5 | 1.5 | 3.0 | 7.2 | 4.3 |
| Mean | −8.5 | −6.2 | 3.1 | 1.1 | 2.1 | 0.6 | 3.4 | 4.4 |
| Standard Deviation | 6.7 | 5.4 | 4.2 | 3.5 | 4.0 | 2.6 | 2.1 | 2.9 |
| Number of Countries | 16 | 16 | 16 | 16 | 16 | 16 | 16 | 16 |

*Source:* Katz (1986a). Based on ILO statistics (see Appendix A).

fact that the rise in services and information is not associated with a decline in industrial occupations constitutes a key difference between development patterns of developed and developing countries.

While the decline in the share of agricultural occupations[9] is uniform throughout the developing world, its rate of decline is quite diverse. There are some countries—such as Argentina, Panama, and the Philippines—where the decreasing trend of the agricultural occupation share is decelerating, while others—such as Egypt and Sri Lanka—have had increases in the rate of change over the last decade.

For the manufacturing occupations, the developing countries show a rise on average of more than 3 percentage points in the 1960s and of 1 point in the 1970s. It is important to note that the higher rise in the 1960s for all countries is mainly due to the double-digit changes that occurred in Iran and Korea. On the other hand, the 1.1 percent change of the 1970s is more consistent throughout the developing world. This pattern can be seen in the lower standard deviation, and is confirmed by Gemmel (1982)—who in his three-sectoral study of the workforce in developing countries, derived a 1.1 percentage change for the industrial sector in 15 developing countries.

The service sector shows also a rise of 2.1 percent in the 1960s and 0.6 percent in the 1970s, which—in both cases—is lower than the rise of industrial occupations' share.

The growth pattern of the information sector is similar to the industrial and service sector, with three significant differences. First, the information sector shows the largest rise in share, both in the 1960s and in the 1970s. Second, the changes are larger in the 1970s than in the 1960s, which is opposite to the trend observed in the manufacturing and service sectors. Third, the differences among developing countries—as measured by the standard deviation—are the smallest among the four sectors, indicating that the trend of an increasing share of information occupations is highly consistent in all developing countries.

In addition, it is important to note that the information sector share in developing countries appears to be increasing much faster than manufacturing. This trend is even more intriguing when we see that the growth of information occupations appears in countries with an important increase in industrial occupations (revealing a process of industrialization)—such as Korea and Syria in the 1970s—as well as countries where industry stagnates—like Chile—or recedes—like Kuwait. This observation would indicate that the growth of information occupations can be associated with diverse factors, among which industrialization is only one of many.

Table 1.7 shows the distribution of information occupation shares in employment for the countries included in Table 1.5, as well as 14 other countries. A brief review of Table 1.7 reveals that an unusually large share of information occupations appear in those countries with an important external trade sector—such as Singapore—or a large tourist trade or financial sector—such as Bermuda, Trinidad and Tobago, and Barbados. In general, countries

**Table 1.7**
**Share of Information Workforce in Developing Countries (c. 1980)**

| Information occupations as percent of total workforce | COUNTRY | FREQUENCY DISTRIBUTION | |
|---|---|---|---|
| | | No. of Countries | Percent of Total Sample |
| 40% or more | Bermuda | 1 | 3 |
| 30% to 39.9% | Costa Rica, Singapore, Trinidad and Tobago | 3 | 8 |
| 20% to 29.9% | Argentina, Bahrain, Barbados, Chile, Cyprus, Hong Kong, Jordan, Kuwait, Panama, Venezuela, Algeria, Mexico | 12 | 33 |
| 10% to 19.9 % | Egypt, El Salvador, Korea, Philippines, Sri Lanka. Syria, Tunisia, Portugal, Seychelles, Guyana, Iran | 11 | 31 |
| 9.9% or less | Cameroon, Colombia, Pakistan, Thailand, Mali, Indonesia, Nepal, Guatemala, India | 9 | 25 |
| All | | 36 | 100 |

*Source:* ILO (1983).

that are relatively small (both in terms of area and population) and highly urbanized (such as Costa Rica and Panama) will tend to have a relatively larger share of information workers. At the other extreme, there are countries where information occupations are low. These are characterized by heavy dependence on agriculture and lower levels of urbanization.

Yet, as previously stated, there are countries with exceptional profiles. Colombia—with 28.5 percent of its economically active population in agriculture—presents an unusually low share of information occupations (9.4 percent). On the contrary, Egypt has 18.6 percent of its labor force in information-related occupations, while the agricultural sector employs 42 percent of the economically active population.

These data provide an indication that the growth of the information sector—as universal as it may be—follows different paths, and must be determined by different independent variables. Figure 1.2 presents different evolutionary patterns for the information sector in the developing world.

Argentina (Figure 1.2a) presents a growing information sector combined with declining industrial occupations. This pattern suggests that information occupations are playing a similar role to that of the service sector in countries that undergo a faltering pace of industrialization. Growth in information

**Figure 1.2**
**Structure of the Workforce in Developing Countries (Four-Sector Aggregation)**

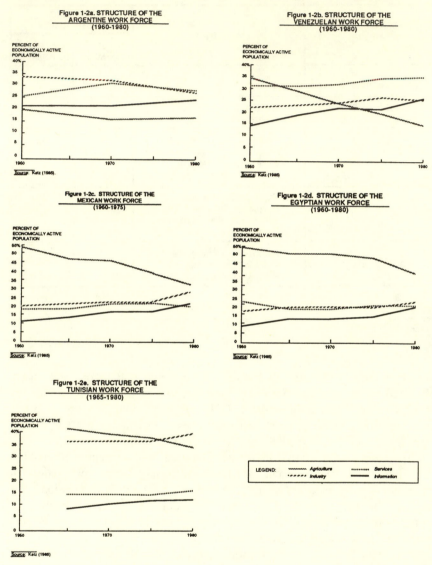

occupations, then, does not respond to increasing demand resulting from the process of industrialization. On the contrary, as we explain later in Chapter 2, it is the result of an unadjusted supply of qualified labor force that keeps on being produced by the educational system and will become a part of the private and public bureaucracies without having a significant impact on productivity and efficiency.

In Venezuela (Figure 1.2b)—in contrast to Argentina—with the exception of the period between 1976 and 1981, all occupational shares except agricultural have been rising since the early 1960s. The decline in industrial occupations registered in the 1981 census is too small to consider a structural change. Data in further years should either confirm or deny this structural trend in the Venezuelan economy.

A trend similar to the Venezuelan can be identified in Mexico (Figure 1.2c), where—again—the industrial, service, and information occupations are growing in share, while the agricultural occupations are decreasing.

Contrary to the Argentine, Venezuelan, and Mexican cases, Egypt (Figure 1.2d) shows a decline in agricultural occupations' share, a stagnation of services, and a rise in industrial and information occupations. The Egyptian information sector has had the highest expansion rate of all occupational shares, achieving only a three-point difference from the industrial sector. The unusually high share of information workers in Egypt is probably a result of increased supply of an educated labor force, rather than demand coming from a stagnating industrial sector. Tunisia (Figure 1.2e) shows the same characteristics as Egypt, except for a stagnating industry.

This brief description shows that, despite the uniform growth of information-intensive occupations throughout the developing world, the pattern of expansion differs. Table 1.8 shows the general trends in each of the four sectors for our sample of 20 developing nations. This summary table raises two issues.

First, the development path that leads to expansion of the information sector in developed countries—mainly the United States (Porat 1976) and the United Kingdom (Wall 1977)—does not seem to be applicable for developing countries. Porat's sequence showed that, in the course of economic development, there is a sequential shift of occupations from agriculture to manufacturing, then services, and finally information. Data in Table 1.8 show a large variety of structural transformations. Although the most logical pattern is that of a declining agricultural share and rising industrial, service, and informational occupations, several countries show an expanding information share and a stagnating or declining share of industrial occupations. Since none of these countries have completely achieved their process of industrialization, the contradicting trends between industrial and information occupations raise a question as to the causes of expansion of the information sector. Namely, why is the information sector growing in developing countries?

Second, whatever the result of the analysis will be, data in Table 1.8 indicate that—contrary to what was hypothesized by Lamberton and Jussawalla (1982)—newly industrializing countries are not leapfrogging from an agricultural economy to an information economy. Jussawalla inferred from World Bank data on the growth of the service sector that the newly industrializing countries (NICs) are becoming information-intensive societies:

**Table 1.8**
**Structural Occupational Changes in Developing Countries, 1960–80**

|            | AGRICULTURE | INDUSTRY | SERVICES | INFORMATION |
|------------|-------------|----------|----------|-------------|
| Argentina  | –           | –        | +        | +           |
| Bahrain    | –           | –        | –        | +           |
| Brazil     | –           | +        | +        | O           |
| Chile      | –           | O        | +        | +           |
| Eqypt      | –           | +        | –        | +           |
| Ghana      | –           | O        | +        | +           |
| Hong Kong  | –           | O        | –        | +           |
| India      | –           | +        | +        | +           |
| Iran       | –           | +        | +        | +           |
| Korea      | –           | +        | +        | +           |
| Kuwait     | O           | –        | –        | +           |
| Mexico     | –           | +        | +        | +           |
| Pakistan   | –           | +        | +        | +           |
| Panama     | –           | +        | +        | +           |
| Philippines| –           | +        | +        | +           |
| Singapore  | –           | +        | –        | +           |
| Sri Lanka  | –           | +        | O        | +           |
| Syria      | –           | +        | O        | +           |
| Tunisia    | –           | +        | O        | +           |
| Venezuela  | –           | +        | +        | +           |

*Legend:* + Increase
o Stagnation
– Decline
*Source:* Compiled by the author based on data from the International Labor Organization.

Development in these countries is fast catching up with the pattern of development in industrialized countries with the NICs leapfrogging into higher growth rates for the service sectors. They are moving into becoming information societies and perhaps should be called Newly Informatics Service Countries. Their industrialization has been overtaken by their services sector. (Jussawalla 1982, 21)

In fact, the only countries that exhibit a combination of declining industry and growing information occupations are Argentina, Bahrain, and Kuwait. While Bahrain and Kuwait should be considered exceptions because of their peculiarity as oil-producing countries, Argentina in the last ten years has exhibited a quite specific phenomenon of deindustrialization—atypical in the developing world.

**Table 1.9**
**Comparative Share of Information and Industrial Occupations**
**in Newly Industrialized Countries (NICs)**

| COUNTRY | YEAR | INFORMATION OCCUPATIONS | INDUSTRIAL OCCUPATIONS |
|---------|------|-------------------------|------------------------|
| Argentina | 1980 | 24.1% | 26.8% |
| Brazil | 1970 | 12.2% | 17.4% |
| Hong Kong | 1980 | 23.5% | 46.0% |
| Korea | 1980 | 14.6% | 26.0% |
| Mexico | 1980 | 20.9% | 27.4% |
| Venezuela | 1980 | 25.6% | 25.0% |

*Source:* Katz (1985).

As shown in Table 1.9, most newly industrialized countries (NICs)—with the exception of Venezuela—show that the workforce engaged in industrial occupations still surpasses the number of information workers. Even if the growth rates for information occupations is higher than for the industrial ones, this relationship is not a reliable indication of the contribution of the information sector to the national product. Due to low productivity levels in the information sector, the industrial sector still remains more important than the information one.

In summary, our empirical data shows that there is no uniform pattern of development of an information sector among developing countries. In fact, data indicates that countries follow different paths of sectoral transformation of their workforce, depending on: (1) the time at which they start to industrialize; (2) the internal economic and political environment; and (3) the country's trade orientation.

## CONCLUSION

Data presented in the course of this chapter showed that there is a uniform growth of information occupations not only throughout the developed world, but also in most developing countries. However, data also supported the hypothesis that the growth patterns of the information workforce differ widely according to each country. While several developing countries follow the most intuitive pattern of declining agricultural share and rising industrial, service, and informational occupations, other developing nations exhibit an expanding information sector as well as a stagnating or declining share of industrial occupations.

Differences in information-sector growth patterns can be related to varying industrialization processes, as in the case of the United States and Britain. In the case of developing countries, nations with an important external trade sector will generally exhibit a relatively large share of information workers. Economics are key. However, in other developing countries, growth of the information sector cannot be explained only by economic factors. Chapter 2 explores the different factors driving information sector growth in developing countries, and compares them with the drivers in developed countries.

## NOTES

1. Another attempt to categorize information workers was Uno (1982), who classified knowledge workers not by the outputs of the industry, but by the informational nature of the work performed.

2. The ISCO 1968 classification includes nine major groups (one-digit codes), 83 minor groups (two-digit codes), 284 unit groups (three-digit codes), and 1,506 occupational categories (five-digit codes) (ILO 1968).

3. For a similar argument in the case of the service sector, see Singlemann (1978).

4. For a disaggregated analysis of the information workforce, see Chapter 2.

5. Reprinted with permission of North Holland Publishing (see Pool et al. 1984).

6. Reprinted with permission of North Holland Publishing (see Jonscher 1983).

7. This work is part of a larger research effort—carried out at the East-West Center in Honolulu, under the direction of M. Jussawalla—which is aimed at measuring the size of the information economy in the countries of the Pacific Basin.

8. Statistics for developing countries were derived using a methodology described in Appendix A.

9. All statistics were calculated considering the total labor force as all employed persons—whether working as employers, self-employed, family workers, or wage/salary earners. This excluded unemployed persons, housewives, full-time students, retired persons, and persons seeking their first job.

# 2

## Explaining Information Workforce Growth in Developing Countries

In Chapter 1, we presented quantitative evidence of the growth of the information workforce in developing countries. But as stated in its conclusion, the key issue remains to be analyzed; namely, what is causing this growth to occur?

In general, economic development is always accompanied by structural changes in the economy. When Clark (1957) conceptually structured the economy in the agricultural, manufacturing, and service sectors, he argued that, as nations became industrialized, a larger proportion of the labor force would pass into manufacturing, because of sectoral differences in productivity. As national incomes rose, there would be a greater demand for services, resulting in an expansion of the service workforce.

Can a similar theory be applied to the information workforce? Is information workforce growth linked to economic progress? Or, are there other non-economic factors affecting expansion? This chapter first reviews the different hypotheses that have been advanced to explain the emergence of an information workforce in the developed world. It then presents a general framework explaining the growth of an information workforce in developing countries. Finally, it supplies quantitative evidence of the role of economic and non-economic variables in the process of information workforce growth.

### INFORMATION SECTOR GROWTH IN DEVELOPED COUNTRIES

When efforts at measuring the service sector started to yield empirical results, three hypotheses explaining the growth of this sector were formu-

An earlier version of this chapter was published in *Telecommunications Policy* (September 1986): 209-28. Reprinted with permission of Butterworth & Co. (London).

lated. Bell explained the growing employment in the service sector in the following terms:

As national incomes rise, one finds, as in the theorem of Christian Engel,...that the proportion of money spent on food at home begins to drop, and the marginal increments are used, first for durables (clothing, housing, automobiles) and then luxury items, recreation, and the like...health and education. (Bell 1973, 128)[1]

These needs—associated with wealth and leisure—can only be satisfied "on the basis of the collective provision of services" (Gershuny 1977). According to Bell, the leading indicator measuring the emergence of the postindustrial society is the growth in the number of service workers. Within the service sector, Bell emphasized the role of scientists, technicians, and professionals as being the key driver for growth.

Bell's hypotheses that the development of the service sector is driven by two factors—increasing final consumption of services, and growth of scientific and technical occupations—have been repeatedly challenged. Gershuny (1977; 1978) argued that, contrary to Engel's theorem, the trend was away from the expenditure on services and toward expenditure of goods. According to Gershuny, the growing employment in the tertiary sector is a manifestation of the increasing division of labor, rather than a change of consumption patterns. Gershuny states that,

as societies develop, the planning, forecasting, and organizational functions are removed from the individual artisans and passed on to other workers, who are not then directly involved in the physical manipulation of materials; hence the growth of "white collar" clerical, administrative, management occupations.... The physical process of production becomes more technical, and so more dependent on those with technological expertise—and indirectly on the educational system which promotes this expertise. (Gershuny 1977, 109)

Gershuny argues, thus, that a large proportion of the service employment is connected with the production process, rather than with the provision of services for final consumption. Following Gershuny, Jonscher argued that

the change...which was responsible for the great majority of information sector growth between (1942 and 1972) was the increase in information service input to the production sector (rather than the increase in the final consumption of information services). (Jonscher 1983, 20)[2]

Jonscher also contradicted Bell's hypothesis that the expansion of the information workforce was driven by the increase in the number of scientific and technical personnel:

While the trends Bell identifies are certainly present, they do not account for the general phenomenon of information work-force expansion. We note...that personnel in education, research and development activities account for only about 15% of the information workforce. Time trend data show that this proportion has in fact been falling during the past three decades,... and that it will continue to fall slightly in the period to 1990. (p. 20)

Thus, Jonscher (1982a; 1982b; 1983) emphasized the importance of the shifts occurring in the manufacturing sector (from production oriented to information related) and minimized the influence of the internal changes occurring in the employment composition of the service sector (from personal services to information-related services). According to Jonscher, the explosion of white collar jobs is essentially due to the growth of a managerial and clerical bureaucracy, which supports production processes.

Consistent with this analysis, Jonscher developed a historical view of the process of expansion of the information sector of the labor force in industrialized countries. He stated that the Industrial Revolution came at a time when limited labor and material resources were the major problem, and technical inefficiency was the main obstacle to economic growth in the developed world. Effective management, and organization and handling of information were relatively less urgent problems.

As technical efficiency increased, the complexity of the economy grew, and the organizational task of coordinating multiple production units became more difficult. At that point, the dominant factors determining output were the efficiency and effectiveness of the information-handling functions of coordination, control, organization, recording, and monitoring. As a result, the economy devised two responses: first, an organizational response—decentralization of management—and, second, a technological one—adoption of information technologies.[3]

Decentralization reduced the complexity of coordinating multiple production tasks. However, this led to an increase in the number of workers engaged in the handling of information. Information technologies—namely, telecommunications and computers—then increased the managers' capabilities of processing and transmitting information. In general, the introduction of information technologies increased the quantity of information that could be processed, on average, by each worker in the information sector.

Concurrently with the notion that changes in industrial structure are the key factors in explaining the growth of the share of information-related occupations, Jonscher showed that the proportion of government staff—public bureaucracy and educational activities—relative to the total information workforce tends to decrease in industrialized countries. According to Jonscher, this is occurring because growth rates of information workers in the private sector (manufacturing and intermediate services) are higher than those in the public sector.[4]

How applicable are these theories to the case of developing countries? Does the decentralization process—as described by Jonscher—occur in the developing world? If so, are changes in the industrial structure the main drivers of information workforce growth?

## INFORMATION SECTOR GROWTH
## IN THE DEVELOPING WORLD

As shown in Chapter 1, the growth of information occupations is highly consistent throughout the developing world. What is driving this increase in the information sector's share of developing country economies? Development theory suggests that, in the course of economic development, there is a sequential shift of employment and material resources from agriculture and other extractive industries to manufacturing and, finally, to services as per capita income rises (Fisher 1933; Clark 1957). This process has been explained in two ways. First, service outputs possess—in aggregate—higher income elasticities of demand than industrial outputs. Therefore, when per capita income rises, industrial outputs will rise faster than service outputs at first, but slower later. Second, since service sector productivity tends to increase more slowly than productivity in manufacturing, a transfer of labor from the industrial to the service sector will be needed at the higher income levels, to maintain the growth rate of service sector outputs (Gemmel 1982).

The rise in the share of the service sector is not homogenous among all types of service industries (Katouzian 1970). Specific services may be expected to increase in importance as industrialization proceeds. According to Katouzian, the distributive services[5] and the producer services are closely linked to the manufacturing industries—their growth resulting from "a rise in demand in a new productive situation" (Katouzian 1970, 366).

These services have been complementary to the growth of manufacturing production in two ways: as complementary factors to urbanization, and as necessary links to the process of round-about or capitalistic production. The growing demand for labour in industrial centers attracted migrants to urban areas, and factor production necessitated a high degree of urbanization. The growth of round-about production increased the range and complexity of intermediate goods and (with the underlying specialization process that was taking place) it helped the conversion of local markets into a unified national market and expanded foreign trade—all demanding services included in this category. Therefore, as the rate of growth of industrial production increased, so did the rate of growth of these services, and vice versa. (Katouzian 1970, 366-67)[6]

Based on Katouzian's findings, Singelmann (1978) hypothesized that the financial, transport, and trade sectors grow in sync with the industrialization process, but stagnate as the economy further develops—possibly declining in a post-industrial society.

The emergence of producer services is a result of increasing specialization of manufacturing establishments and their complex organization. As pointed out by Fuchs (1968), Gershuny (1978), and Jonscher (1982b), activities such as accounting or advertising once were performed within the organizations at earlier stages of industrial development, and their emergence as separate industries is tied in with the development of economies of scale (see also Machlup 1962, 39-40).

A third factor explaining the growth of the service sector is that of the expansion of government and its increased influence on the economy. This factor is particularly relevant when analyzing the expansion of social services. Katouzian (1970) links the emergence of these industries to the growth of per capita income, which leads in turn to mass consumption. Singelmann considers that, more appropriately,

While [these services] do cater to the individual, their emergence is only partly the result of individual demand. More important for their growth is the collective demand, at least in industrialized countries, in terms of the idea of social welfare, health standards, and other social legislation. It follows, therefore, that social services are less oriented toward individualistic demands but rather toward individuals as a collective entity, be it the neighborhood, the community, the state or even the nation. (Singelmann 1978, 33)

As a result, the expansion of these industries is largely a function of public policies—which, in turn, result from the specific outcome of competing interests in the realm of state action. As Singelmann (1978) states, "The social service sector is an important manifestation of the role of the state in society" (p. 33).

Consequently, the provision of certain services—such as education—is linked to the existence of group demand, which can appear at very low levels of economic development. Even if a country is at early stages of development, group demands—enhanced by political actions—result in a strong pressure on the supply of these services. Thus, service employment can be relatively substantial even if the income per capita is low, because of group demand expressed through political structures.

Other factors have also been noted as playing an important role in explaining changes in the workforce structure of developing nations. Bairoch (1977) explains the changes by the effect of exogenous factors. He considers that, for more than a century, the Third World has been in an active economic relationship with the industrialized nations, with the net result that the developing economies have been distorted. Bairoch believes that one of the symptoms of this distortion is the hypertrophy of the service sector. According to Bairoch,

although in 1960 Third World economy, measured by the percentage of the labour force employed in agriculture was at the same level as that of the industrialized countries of Western Europe and North America around 1819, the Third World possessed the same proportion of persons employed in trade and banking as had been reached by the industrialized countries around 1890. (Bairoch 1977, 161)[7]

Interestingly enough, the transport and communication sector in the 1960 developing economies showed a level of development corresponding to the period of 1840–50 in Europe and North America. On the other hand, the proportion of the labor force engaged in the manufacturing and extractive industries was lower than it was in the industrialized countries in 1800. Bairoch considers that the high level of tertiary employment can be explained by the

excessive development of commercial activity and public services in most of the countries concerned and by the impossibility of absorbing in the secondary sector all the surplus labor from agriculture. (p. 161)

This point has been supported empirically by Katouzian (1970), Bhalla (1973), and also conceptually by Rada (1981). The growth of the service sector in developing countries is therefore the result of not only indigenous factors—such as the industrialization process and sector differentials—but also of external distortions in the industrialization process itself.

While the theories presented above did not deal specifically with an information workforce, some of their formulations are helpful in formulating a theory of information workforce growth in the developing world, to be presented in the next section.

## A HYPOTHETICAL MODEL

Changes in the employment structure of a national economy can be of two kinds: (1) employment shifts among the three industrial sectors, often referred to as a "sectoral" shift; or (2) changes in the internal composition of each industry sector itself, named a "compositional" shift. The former are more likely to reflect the impact of changes in demand and investment patterns on employment growth, while the latter would more typically result from changes in the technology and organizational structure within industries.

Since the introduction of new technology and the changes in organizational structure are more recent trends in developing countries, shifts in demand would remain the primary factor explaining information sector growth. Therefore, the increase in demand for information workers is linked to, among other variables, changes in the demand for manufactured goods. Growth in demand would be only a function of the need to increase the efficiency in the production of goods and services, without modifying the existing capacity.

However, in the case of developing countries, a demand function of this nature cannot explain—alone—the growth of information occupations' share of the total workforce. Research (Singelmann 1978; Sabolo, Gaude, and Wery 1975; Katouzian 1970) shows that certain information-intensive industries tend to expand in developing countries independently from the process of industrialization. Some service industries (such as banking, financial services, telecommunications, consulting, and advertising) expand as a result of the process of industrialization, while others (such as government) tend to grow—at least in terms of employment—due to reasons other than economic ones.

**Figure 2.1**
**Information Sector Growth in Developing Countries**

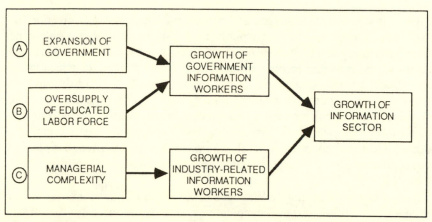

*Source:* Author.

It is our hypothesis that the expansion of the information sector in developing countries has to be jointly explained by two demand functions and a supply function, and integrated within the conceptual framework illustrated in Figure 2.1. The expanding role of governments (A) in developing countries will drive the growth in the number of government information workers (demand function). The specification of a supply function such as (B) refers to the effects of a dysfunctional education system—as well as traditional factors such as rural-urban migration—on the balance of labor supply and demand. Finally, (C) represents the demand function that was developed for industrialized nations. The following sections discuss these three factors in detail, and show their varying importance in causing information sector growth in the developing world.

## Expansion of Governments

Ever since the formulation of the "law of expanding state expenditures" by Adolph Wagner in the second half of the nineteenth century, economists and specialists in public finance have been concerned with the interaction between processes of economic growth and expansion of the state. According to a modern formulation of Wagner's original law, it is considered that,

as per capita income rises in industrializing nations, their public sectors will grow in relative importance [due to the following reasons]: Firstly, an expansion would come about with respect to the administrative and protective functions of the state ... because of the substitution of public for private activity. In addition, new needs for public, regulative and protective activity would develop as a result of increased complexity of legal relationships and communications that inevitably accompanied the greater division of labour with industrialization. (Bird 1971, 2)

Wagner also identified "the increase in population density and urbanization" as a factor that would cause growth in public expenditures in order to maintain the existing efficiency level within growing urban environments. He also predicted that an increase in real income would lead to an expansion of educational, cultural, and leisure expenditures, since "the income-elasticity of demand for these services was greater than unity." Finally, due to technological innovation, the amount of capital required to adopt certain technologies could only be financed by the state. Based on time series of aggregate expenditures for selected developed countries, several authors have confirmed Wagner's law in its general formulation (Musgrave 1969; Bird 1971; Gupta 1967; Goffman and Mahar 1971).[8]

In other words, according to Wagner's law, growth of government is due to the new societal needs "for public regulative and protective activity." Given this assumption, a redistribution of state expenditures should occur aimed at allocating more funds to social, environmental, and administrative services (Rose 1976). This second reallocating process, which parallels that of the expanding role of the state, is particularly important in determining information and communications development.

Statistics presented by Bird (1971) show that the most rapid expenditure increases have generally been in either the social services (health, education, and welfare) or environmental services (transportation, communication, and natural resources). Expenditures in administration did not seem to rise— contrary to what Wagner predicted.

A similar phenomenon has been identified by other contemporary economists. For example, Kusnetz analyzed data on the industrial structure of several countries, and identified the growing importance of governments in the supply of basic services. Kusnetz stated that,

the growing urbanization of the developed economies has meant much greater demand for labor-consuming services of urban governments (in police, sanitation, public health, education, and the like), while the growing complexity of the country's productive system has led to an increase in the supervisory and regulatory functions of central governments. (Kusnetz 1966, 150)

Similarly, Galbraith established the growing economic role of the state:

The industrial system...has extended its influence deeply into the state. Those policies that are vital for the industrial system—regulation of aggregate demand, maintenance of the large public (if preferably technical) sector on which this regulation depends, underwriting of advanced technology and provision of an increasing volume of trained and educated manpower—are believed to be of the highest social urgency. (Galbraith 1968, 327)

According to these authors, as a result of changes in the economic and demographic structures, the state increasingly expands and changes its activities in order to better foster economic growth.

Kohl (1983) provided additional evidence of this reallocation process over the last century. By means of extended time series for eight Western European countries, he shows the variable rates of growth in different government functions. He provided evidence of the existence of the redistribution process of government expenditures:

—From as far back as data sources go until about 100 years ago, the defining activities of the state (defense of its territory, maintenance of internal order, mobilization of finance) absorbed the largest share of total expenditures.

—Even prior to World War I, however, a slow but continuous trend toward an increasing share of public expenditure for social purposes began....

—[Finally,] in 1970 no Western European central government spent less than forty percent of its resources on social services (including education). [Conversely,] expenditures for the military have declined to about ten percent more or less, and expenditure shares for general financial and judicial administration are even smaller. (Kohl 1983, 205)[9]

Kohl's findings reconfirm Bird's statistics on rapid expenditure increases in social and environmental services. It is important to point out that the category of "economic and environmental services," which includes communications as one of the public expenditure items, tends to grow in relative terms in seven out of eight European countries analyzed by Kohl—the only exception being Denmark. Moreover, if we assume that most state functions and services are information intensive (education, social services, economic and environmental services, and administration), increased state activity will necessarily imply the expansion of the information sector. If we assume that developing nations are undergoing processes of economic growth similar to those of nineteenth-century Europe, the expansion of the information sector in developing countries appears—at least partially—to be a logical consequence of the expanding role of the state in the economy.

For historical reasons, the phenomenon of state expansion is even more important in the developing world. Government size in developing countries tends to be comparatively larger than that of industrialized countries when they had similar levels of development. Both Dahrendorf (1967) and Gerschenkron (1952) examined this tendency among European countries, while Collier and Messick (1975) found evidence of its existence in the developing world. The historical role of the state in the economy of many developing countries has been quite different from that of most industrialized nations (a notable exception being France). In most developing countries, the state—through its administrative machine—plays an incomparably greater role in the economy than the state in developed countries before the advent of industrialization.

This phenomenon is due to a variety of reasons. First, the governments of the Third World are under pressure to provide their constituencies with services that were nonexistent for developing countries during the Industrial Revolution. Second, research evidence (Thomas et al. 1979; Thomas and Meyer 1980) shows that the effort to mobilize people in developing countries promotes expansion of the government's bureaucratic structures. Finally, Modelski (1978) and Bergensen and Schoenberg (1980) have demonstrated that state formation processes are linked to long cycles of economic competition and political hegemony in the world system. According to this argument,

The breakdown of growth and hegemony ... is accompanied by interstate conflict and organizational expansion of the state apparatus. (Thomas and Meyer 1980, 475)

As a result of these three factors, compared to developed countries the state expands faster in developing countries at lower levels of development. As a result, at least in the first stages of development, the expansion of the state may be the main factor explaining the growth of the information workforce.

### Oversupply of Information Workers

Change in the share of information occupations in the developing world can also be the result of an increase in the supply of labor due to population pressure, as well as the oversupply of an educated labor force.

Information workers are generally trained individuals with a higher level of education than the average worker. Consequently, there is a high correlation between the level of education in the labor supply and total information workers. In developing nations, educational systems tend to train a higher number of workers than the productive systems can absorb. Within this context, governments act as employers compensating for the dysfunctionality of the educational system. The consequence is inefficiency—the overcrowding of government offices, without commensurate productive activity.

The government in developing countries tends to act as a compensating mechanism at two levels. First, state and local government will tend to grow in order to partially offset rural-urban migration. Second, central government will tend to grow beyond its needs in order to absorb the increased supply of information workers—migrated as well as city born.

If expansion of the information sector is a function of the capacity of the government to absorb educated labor, it could be hypothesized that this growth will not be constant, but rather a function of specific political factors. For example, it can be suggested that authoritarian regimes are better able and willing to control the social demands expressed by unemployed information workers, and therefore will tend less to use the state as a mechanism to absorb an excess information workforce. Conversely, democratic regimes in developing countries—which depend on satisfied constituencies—will tend to utilize the government as a means of meeting social demands, and therefore are likely to hire information workers beyond the needs of managing the public good.

### Industrialization and Division of Labor

In addition to the impact of government expansion and the oversupply of information workers, industrialization plays a significant role, particularly in the newly industrialized countries (NICs). A process similar to the one described by Jonscher (1982a, 1982b, 1983) for the developed countries may well be taking place in industrializing countries. However, a caveat should be introduced at this point. While Jonscher's argument linking diffusion of information technologies to the need for organizational efficiency remains valid for developing countries, his description of the sequence that led to the diffusion of information technologies may not apply in the same way.

Two hypotheses can be formulated. First, in developing countries where information technologies are available at the same time that industries are beginning to strive for technical efficiency, decentralization does not have to be a natural outcome of managerial complexity (as argued for the developed countries). Information technologies can help managers in developing countries to maintain greater control without having to delegate decisions. This hypothesis is supported by the research literature that associates diffusion of information technologies with a lack of decentralization, and the consequent lack of growth in information workers. Information technology makes the management of complex structures more feasible, resulting in less division of labor among managers and other clerical personnel.[10]

A second contradicting hypothesis would be that decentralization could be fostered by the introduction of information technologies. Burlingame (1961) and Pfeffer and Leblevici (1977) have proved that information technologies lead to decentralization and, therefore, to an increase in the number of clerical and managerial workers. In an analysis of 37 small manufacturing companies, Pfeffer and Lebevici (1977) found that, with size statistically controlled, there was a negative relationship between information technology and centralization. The more computers were adopted by an organization, the larger the number of its managers and clerks in different units. Thus, according to this finding, we could argue that, in developing countries, information technologies would increase the growth of the information sector—and not the other way around.[11] However, this hypothesis remains at the initial stage of formulation and needs further empirical analysis to be validated.

In addition to the expansion of government, other factors promote the growth of the information sector at early stages of development. Countries that base their first phase of economic growth on the export of raw materials and foodstuffs will tend to develop a transport and communications infrastructure, as well as social overhead facilities essential for fostering other manufacturing activities. These are the economic forward linkages of extractive industries—

which also result in the development of a banking and financing system (Caves and Holton 1959). This results in the expansion of the producer and distributive services in the first phases of development. This conclusion can easily be proved by analyzing the input-output tables of developing countries, and determining the value added by the external trade sector to the gross domestic product.

### Historical Model of Causality

A general model for explaining the growth of the information sector can be derived from the theoretical assumptions described above: While the information sector tends to expand in almost all countries and at almost all levels of development (until it reaches 50 percent share of total employment), factors influencing that growth are different according to two developmental stages.

In the first stage of development—referred to as state-building—the main force behind the growth of the information sector is the expansion of the government. This process is driven by two objectives: (1) the formation of a political and institutional framework aimed at supporting economic growth; and (2) the provision of social services to the population. As a result, the state-building stage focuses on the formation or restructuring of a bureaucratic administration in the Weberian sense—with clearly defined roles on a judicial, financial, and administrative level. In addition to the growth in administrative employment, the need to provide basic services—such as public education, communications, and transport—has a direct impact on the share of information occupations in the total workforce.

In the second stage—as a result of the process of industrialization and economic growth—the need for specialization and division of labor becomes the main variable explaining information sector expansion. At this point, while the government sector continues expanding, it grows at a slower rate than the information sector as a whole. This feature is what led Jonscher to argue that, in the United States, "The growth of the information work-force must still be reckoned as predominantly a private rather than a public sector phenomenon" (Jonscher 1983, 20).[12] At this time, it is the private sector that becomes the main contributor to the expansion of the information workforce.

This general process tends to vary from country to country. While industrialized countries have followed the two stages in a more or less linear fashion, developing countries tend to face the challenge of state-building and industrialization simultaneously. It is precisely the simultaneity of the processes of economic and political development in developing countries that can hide the importance of the political system as a factor in explaining the expansion of the information sector.

## SOME QUANTITATIVE EVIDENCE

As explained above, most studies of the growth of the information sector in developed countries emphasized economic growth as its main determinant. We

**Figure 2.2**
**Information Sector Size vs. GNP per Capita for 45 Countries, c. 1980**

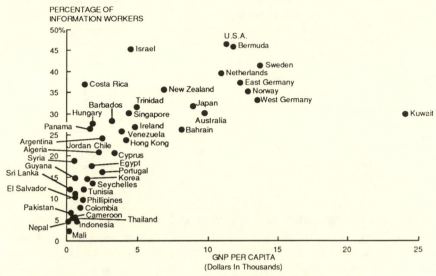

*Source:* Data from ILO (1982), and World Bank (1982), analysis by the author.

argued, however, that, for developing countries, demand emerging from indus-try could not by itself explain the changes occurring in the occupational struc-ture. Figure 2.2 constitutes the first piece of evidence supporting the notion that other functions besides industry-related demand drive information sector growth, particularly at lower levels of development. The figure presents a scattergram of per capita GNP (in U.S. dollars) and size of the information workforce (measured in percentage points) for 45 countries at the beginning of this decade. The scattergram shows a general curvilinear pattern—according to which the information sector tends to expand at a very high pace at lower levels of development, and then to stabilize at levels between 35 percent and 45 percent of the economically active population. The line reveals a very good fit when data on information sector share (Y) is regressed against per capita GNP (X), according to a multiplicative model, such as the following:

$$Y = a X * b$$

The regression yields the following estimates and $R^2$:

$$Y = 0.48 X * (-0.81)$$
$$R^2 = 0.727$$

While acknowledging the danger of inferring a historical trend from a cross-sectional sample, data and equation results would suggest that there are other

**Table 2.1**
**Information Sector Size and Industry Share of GDP for Selected Countries, 1980**

| Country | Information Workers Share of Active Population | Industrial Sector Share of GDP |
|---------|-----------------------------------------------|--------------------------------|
| Egypt | 18.6% | 35.0% |
| Jordan | 21.3% | 32.0% |
| Venezuela | 25.6% | 47.0% |
| Algeria | 20.7% | 57.0% |
| Hungary | 27.4% | 59.0% |

*Source:* Katz (1986a, 1986b); World Bank (1983).

factors causing information sector growth at lower levels of development. Countries like Egypt and Jordan exhibit an information workers' share that does not necessarily seem to respond to demands for efficiency emerging from their respective industrial sectors, which are quite small (see Table 2.1). In general terms, for relatively equal information workers' share, the industry share of GDP varies widely across countries.

**Figure 2.3**
**Structure of the Information Sector, Korea, 1960–81**

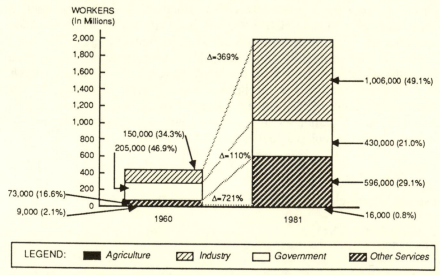

*Source:* Data from ILO (1965, 1982); Heller and Tait (1983); analysis by the author.

An unusually high share of information workers at lower levels of development can only be explained by differentiating the factors of growth and the type of worker. The hypothetical historical model presented above argued that, at lower levels of development, the expansion of government and the oversupply of educated labor force are the dominant drivers of information sector growth, while, at higher levels of development, the industrialization process takes precedence.

Two pieces of evidence have been generated to support this hypothesis. In the first place, we analyzed the internal composition of the information workforce of two developing countries at two points in time: 1960 and 1980. Figure 2.3 presents the internal composition of the Korean information sector, according to an industrial breakdown. It shows the changes occurring in the profile of the information sector between 1960—when the government was the dominant source of growth—and 1981—when manufacturing and services constituted the core of demand for information workers. While government employees represented 46.9 percent of the information workforce in 1960, their share decreased 25.9 percent in 1981. The most important shift in share occurred from the government sector to the industrial and service sectors. The growth rate of information workers allocated to industry between 1960 and 1981 was 721 percent, and that of government information workers was 110 percent, while the growth rate of the sector as a whole was 369 percent.

The Egyptian case (see Figure 2.4) enables us to make a comparison between the changes in the internal structure of the information workforce in a

**Figure 2.4**
**Structure of the Information Sector, Egypt, 1960–81**

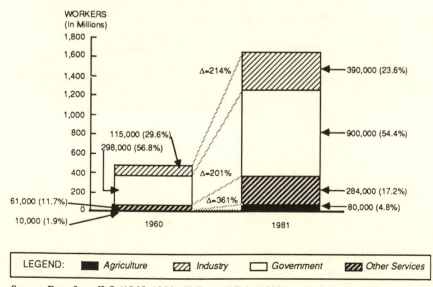

LEGEND: ■ Agriculture ▨ Industry □ Government ▨ Other Services

*Source:* Data from ILO (1965, 1982); Heller and Tait (1983); analysis by the author.

newly industrialized country (Korea) and a developing country (Egypt). In the Egyptian case, the government information workers represent more than half of the sector, even after 19 years. Despite the fact that the industrial information workers have grown at a faster pace (361 percent) than the information sector as a whole (214 percent), the government information workers still remain the major portion of the information sector.[13] The Egyptian case supports the hypothesis that, at lower levels of development, the expansion of government is the main contributor to the growth of the information sector.

The importance of government expansion in explaining information sector growth at earlier stages of development was also underlined in two studies of the information sector of developing economies. Vitro's (1984) analysis shows that 50.3 percent of the contribution of the information sector to the Venezuelan GDP emanates from general government activities. In a significantly lower estimate, Jussawalla and Chee-Wah-Cheah (1982) estimated that government services represented 20.9 percent of the information sector in Singapore, when the share was measured by value added to GDP.

The percentage difference between Venezuela and Singapore might be explained by different historical traditions in terms of state intervention. Singapore is a city-state that has devised a development strategy based on international trade and export of services, coupled with a low degree of state intervention in the economy; it is aimed at becoming a financial center of Southeast Asia. On the other hand, Venezuela's statist policies have become a main factor in the expansion of the state's intervention in the economy, as is the case in most Latin American countries. Public bureaucracies in various Latin American countries are generally growing in size, and extending their influence over many different sectors of civil society. In Venezuela, since the government nationalized the oil industry in 1976, the public sector has accounted for 60 percent of the gross domestic product, and now directs more than 200 agencies and companies.

In conclusion, in addition to the vast expansion of the public sector into new activities linked to its increasing intervention in the economy, government activities and operations in developing countries have grown in complexity and specialization. The expansion into new areas has led to the establishment of new activities. The need for coordination of these new activities has resulted in further increases in the number of personnel required.

The second piece of evidence supporting the hypothetical role of government in explaining information sector growth consists of differentiating the shares of government information workers (A) and industrial information workers (B), and regressing both indicators against the level of economic development, as measured by per capita GNP (C). It is assumed that if (A) is weakly related to (C), then the overall growth of the information sector at low levels of development is driven mostly by growth of (A)—which is what we showed in the first piece of evidence.

**Figure 2.5**
**Government Information Workers vs. GNP, 1980**

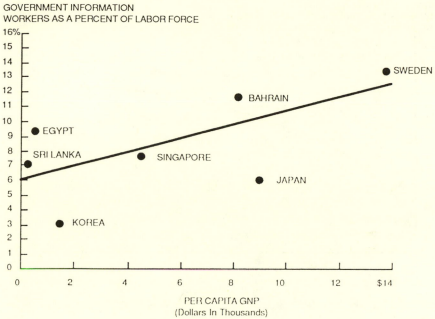

*Source:* Data from ILO (1982), Heller and Tait (1983), World Bank (1982); analysis by the author.

From a statistical standpoint, the growth of government information workers is almost completely independent from economic development. A simple linear regression (see Figure 2.5) between the share of government information workers (A) and per capita GNP (C) yields the following results:

A = .0004 (C) + 6.0085
$R^2$ = 0.0389

The weak relationship was also proved by Heller and Tait (1983), when they found no correlation between the size of government (as measured by the number of employees) and national income.

In contrast, the curvilinear regression of industry-related information workers (B) with national income (C) yields a high $R^2$ (see Figure 2.6):

B = 0.39 (C)* (– 1.63)
$R^2$ = 0.866

**Figure 2.6**
**Industry-Related Information Workers vs. GNP, 1980**

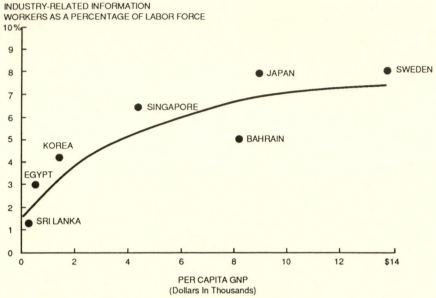

INDUSTRY-RELATED INFORMATION
WORKERS AS A PERCENTAGE OF LABOR FORCE

PER CAPITA GNP
(Dollars In Thousands)

*Source:* Data from ILO (1982), Heller and Tait (1983), World Bank (1982); analysis by the author.

As expected, the higher the level of per capita income (taken as an indicator of economic development), the larger the proportion of information workers allocated to the industrial sector.

Data appear to indicate that there are two factors determining growth of the information sector: (1) the process of industrialization, and (2) the expansion of governments. Economic development is clearly determining the expansion of industry-related information workers, while this is not the case for government information workers.

The hypothetical model presented in the previous section explains that the importance of political and economic factors in determining information sector growth varies historically. The limited evidence presented here appears to support this hypothesis. Indeed, data show that, while the expansion of government is the main reason for information sector growth at lower levels of development, the need to increase efficiency in the service and industrial sectors will appear as the main explanatory variable at later stages of economic growth. Consequently, newly industrializing countries—such as Korea—will tend to exhibit information-sector growth patterns that are closer to the ones found in industrialized societies.

In addition, data do not disprove the supply function presented in the previous section. According to this function, change in the share of information occupations in the developing world can also be the result of an increase in the supply of labor due to population pressure, as well as the oversupply of an educated labor force by a dysfunctional education system.

Within this context of oversupply of information workers, the government acts as a compensating mechanism at two levels. First, state and local government in the developing world will tend to grow, in order to partially counter rural-urban migration. Second, the central government will tend to grow beyond its needs, in order to absorb the increased supply of information workers and better control social demands emerging from unemployed information workers.

## CONCLUSION

Chapter 2 showed that, in general, the growth of the information workforce in developing countries is driven by the combined impact of three factors: first, the growth of the government sector, in a need to support delivery of basic services. In addition, the expansion of governments is magnified by the role played by the state absorbing the surplus of educated labor that cannot be employed in the private sector. Finally, industrialization may play a significant role, by requiring information workers to organize and manage increasingly complex production processes.

It has also been suggested in Chapter 2 that the relative importance of each of the three factors varies according to two developmental stages. In the first stage of economic and political development, the main force behind the growth of the information sector is the expansion of the government. In the second stage, as a result of the process of industrialization and economic growth, the need for information workers to manage the production of goods becomes the main variable driving information workforce growth.

In sum, Part I has explored the role played by governments in the growth of the information workforce. Part II will analyze the influence of the political system on the process of diffusion of information technologies.

## NOTES

1. This explanation was also shared to a certain degree by Parker and Porat, who explained the transition toward information societies: "A second reason may be the satiation or leveling off of some physical needs with a consequent shift in new demand to concern with style, atmosphere or other intangible (i.e., information-related) attributes of consumption, or a direct demand to information products and services" (1975, 11).

2. This and the following excerpt are reprinted with permission of North-Holland Publishing (see Jonscher 1983).

3. For a detailed description of the organizational response, see Chandler (1977).

4. The Expert Group set up by the OECD's Information, Computer, and Communications Working Party had previously included the views shared by Jonscher within a more comprehensive framework. The group stated that the increase in the employment share of information workers was determined by "the combined impact of changes in the distribution of employment between industries and in the occupational composition of employment within each industry" (OECD 1981, 45).

As a result, the OECD's Expert Group mentioned three factors explaining information sector growth:

• the shift in employment toward the service sector and away from agriculture and manufacturing;

• the internal changing composition occurring within the service sector employment; and

• the substitution of information for noninformation labor in the manufacturing sector.

5. Singelmann (1978) developed a disaggregated scheme for analyzing differential growth patterns within the service sector. According to this author, this sector is composed of the following subsectors and industries:

• Distributive services (transportation, communication, and trade industries);

• Producer services (banking, financing, accounting, and legal services, among others);

• Social services; and

• Personal services.

6. Reprinted with permission of the publisher (see Katouzian 1970).

7. This and the following excerpt are reprinted with permission of the publisher and Methuen and Co. (see Bairoch 1977).

8. For a review of this research body, see Cameron (1978), Peacock and Wiseman (1967), and Taylor (1983).

9. Reprinted with permission of the publisher (see Kohl 1983).

10. As Thompson (1967) stated, one of the reasons for the division of labor in organizations is limitations of cognitive capacity.

11. This effect—identified at a micro level—does not necessarily have to be valid at a macro level (the risk of the "ecological" fallacy).

12. Reprinted with permission of North-Holland Publishing (see Jonscher 1983).

13. The role of the government in the Egyptian economy is enormous. According to Ahmed (1984), the state accounts for 54 percent of GDP, 40 percent of total employment, and 70 percent of total investment in the economy.

# PART II

# DIFFUSION OF INFORMATION TECHNOLOGIES IN THE DEVELOPING WORLD: A MATTER OF POLITICS RATHER THAN MARKETS

Four major trends have been identified as composing the phenomenon of emergence of the information society: emergence of a sizable information workforce, increased diffusion of information technologies, growth of societal information flows, and expansion of information industries. Part II focuses on the analysis of the diffusion of information technologies. Its main argument is that diffusion of information technologies in developing countries is strongly influenced by political factors, such as nation-building imperatives, industrial policies, or protection of government-owned telecommunication services from competition arising from cost-effective substitute technologies.

This part is structured in four chapters. In the first, chapter 3, we review the theories and research efforts aimed at understanding the process of diffusion of information technologies. We conclude that political variables have been either ignored or superficially considered when explaining technological diffusion. In response to this, we present the main tenets of a theory that emphasizes the role of politics in conditioning the process of diffusion of information technologies.

Evidence provided in support of this theory is of a varied nature—both quantitative and qualitative. The methodologies used range from multivariate regression analysis and descriptive statistical analysis, to the study of qualitative data. In our second chapter, chapter 4, we show how regulatory pricing mechanisms can shape the process of technological substitution between different media, and have a direct impact on the volume of information flow. Chapter 5 analyzes how government policy has an influence on the rate of diffusion of information technologies. Finally, Chapter 6 explores the political nature of the process of intercountry diffusion of information technologies.

# 3

# Politics as a Driver of Information Technology Diffusion

Evidence of the relation between economic growth and the diffusion of information technologies[1]—whether mass communications, telecommunications, or computing—can be found throughout the research literature (Hudson et al. 1979). Specifically, media consumption (for example, purchase of newspapers, radios, and TV sets) has been related to the general population's structure of demand (Lerner 1958; Bain 1962). Likewise, the supply and demand of telecommunications have been linked to the level of economic development of a country (Jipp 1963; CCITT 1972; Schapiro 1976; Hardy 1980; Pierce and Jequier 1982). Similarly, diffusion of computers has been related to the development of the nonagricultural sector of the economy (Han 1978; Stoneman 1976; and Chow 1967). However, the deployment and expansion of a vast portion of the information technologies infrastructure cannot be adequately explained solely by market mechanisms or simple economic variables.

The expansion of the telecommunications network in most countries of the world, the adoption of new transmission technologies (such as satellites and fiber optics), and the expansion of a great portion of the infrastructure of supply of media messages—all are processes driven by public policy, and are therefore shaped by political factors as well as economic forces. Thus, while correlation exists between economic development and the diffusion of information technologies, some of the relationships between the economic system and the information and communications system are mediated by the political system. In fact, in some cases, diffusion of information technologies can be entirely the result of needs emerging from the political system—having little or nothing to do with market mechanisms.

Despite the importance of political factors in determining diffusion of information technologies, not enough research has been done regarding the dialectic interaction between those technologies and the political system.[2] We are concerned here with two issues: (1) the role of information technologies in the process of political development (defined as the process that leads to the emergence of nationality and the buildup of the state), and (2) the relation between the state and the promotion of industrial policies resulting in the diffusion of information technologies. In the first case, we are asking to what extent information technology contributes or hinders the process of state-building. In the second, we seek to identify the role of the state in shaping processes of diffusion of information technologies.

With regard to the first issue, the research literature has shown that: (1) media can be used to increase political participation and build political allegiances (Lerner 1958; Pool 1963); (2) domestic mail traffic is an appropriate indicator of political integration and nation building (Deutsch 1957); and (3) telecommunications have been successfully used for integrating national territories by fighting geographical isolation (Deutsch 1957; Claval 1980).

It seems to us, however, that these findings have only scratched the surface of the complex relationship that links information technologies to the state, particularly at the stage of state-building. In fact, they provide partial empirical evidence of the existence of a relationship, without integrating it within a comprehensive causal framework that includes both political and economic variables.

With regard to the second issue, the scholarly literature has only recently started to identify processes by which, in the absence of any preexisting pressure from local capitalistic forces, the state temporarily emerges as "a relatively autonomous actor which helps shape the development of local productive forces" (Evans 1985), and fosters the development of an information industry. Indeed, research on the autonomous role of the state in driving the diffusion of information technologies is still in its infancy.

In order to start defining a theory that provides a comprehensive framework of the role of information within the process of political development and of the role of politics in shaping the emergence of information industry, it is first necessary to identify the relevant elements in a theory of the state. In that sense, this chapter focuses on *why* the state intervenes so heavily in the process of diffusion of information technologies. It is less concerned with the mechanisms of state intervention than with the reasons for such action. While our subject is developing countries, we sometimes use examples of developed countries to substantiate our conclusions.

Section 1 reviews the social sciences literature to determine the role attributed by different theoretical bodies and traditions to political factors in the diffusion of information technologies. Section 2 proposes an overall comprehensive framework of causality—including both political and economic variables. Section 3 is addressed to our first specific issue: the role of information technologies within the process of state-building. Likewise, section 4 focuses on answering the second of our two issues: the impact of industrial policies on the process of diffusion of information technologies. Finally, based on the findings of the previous sections, section 5 centers on the critical questions for today's policymakers. We explore the future role of the state in the information technology field in developing countries. For example, will Third World countries ever deregulate their information industries—the way some industrialized nations are doing? What are the major trends with regard to political intervention in the transition toward information societies?

## EXPLAINING THE DIFFUSION OF INFORMATION TECHNOLOGIES: ALTERNATIVE THEORIES

### Early Theoretical Models

The intellectual origins of a theory explaining the role of information and communication within social systems can be traced to general macrohistorical models that make a distinction between society and community. Despite the fact that none of these models included the notion of information as such, they implicitly formulated a theory of information, communications, and society. These early models focused mainly on the role of information in social communities, rather than discussing the reasons for diffusion of information technologies.

The early interpretations of processes of social change are almost exclusively built around the contrast between tradition and modernity. Early social theory constructs were developed in order to analyze the characteristics of traditional and modern societies, and explain the mechanisms of change. Toennies was the first theorist to conceive a theory that reified a dichotomy between community and society (Lerner 1976). Strongly influenced by the philosophy of history[3]— which started to develop with Hegel and continued with Marx—Toennies conceived human history as an irreversible trend from community to society. For Toennies, history can be defined as

a trend (tendency) from the original (simple, family-like) communism and the (rural-urban) individualism which emanates from it and is based thereon, to the independent (metropolitan-universalistic) individualism and the thereby determined (national and international) socialism. (Toennies 1971, 5)

A similar dichotomy was later defined by Weber using the terms *Vergemeinschaftung* ("communalisation") and *Vergessellschaftung* ("sociation").[4] *Vergemeinschaftung* is based on a sense of solidarity with others—for example, kinship relations, the feeling of affinity among professional colleagues, or the code of conduct observed by members of an aristocracy. *Vergesellschaftung*—on the contrary—is based on considerations of material advantage, irrespective of personal or social obligations.

Similar dichotomies were defined by Henri Maine (1885) (distinction between status and contract), and Durkheim (1893) (distinction between mechanical and organic solidarity). Durkheim's merit was to focus on the survival of the small group cemented by "organic" solidarity but immersed in a society made of "mechanical ties."

Classical views of society—those originating with Marx (1969) and Toennies (1971), and refined by Weber (1946) and Durkheim (1893)—were consistent in the sense that they used their respective dichotomies as ideal types and that they considered actual societies to contain elements of both types. In that sense, every citizen belongs to a plurality of communities—such as family, class, or nation—each of which is linked by different types of relationships or solidarities.

The notion of information—as such—does not appear in any of these early historical models. Yet, its implicit reference can be identified. In a more or less explicit way, all major macrosociological theories are theories of communication, because—by referring to the multiplicity of linkages that relate the individual to society—they take into account the connectivities and information flows that occur within any societal context.

Weber—for example—expressed that, among the cultural elements that provide the basis for the formation of a nation, one must consider "a common language," a national literature, and newspapers (Weber 1946, 178). For example, he explains that

Today, quite considerable pecuniary and capitalist interests are anchored in the maintenance and cultivation of the popular language: the interest of the publishers, editors, and authors and...above all, newspapers. Once Polish and Latvian newspapers existed, the language fight conducted by governments or ruling strata of another language community had become as good as hopeless, *for reasons of state are powerless against these forces*. (Weber 1946, 179, emphasis added by the author)

Weber considered information shared by means of a common language and a communications technology (the press) as being a determinant factor in the emergence of nationalism.

Toennies' notion of public opinion is fairly consistent with Weber's concept of language and communications technology:

Patriotic-political judgements, to be sure, claim universal validity much more rarely. Their intention is to be subjective; they are supposed to express the emotions and the manner of thinking of a people, especially of a politically organized nation, regarding matters that do not concern other nations, do not interest them, and presumably are not understood by them; or that are necessarily negatively evaluated by those whose interests and modes of thinking are likely to be opposed to one's own. (Toennies 1971, 252-53)

It is clear, then, that among early social theorists, information was conceived as part of the cultural cement of political communities. Information technologies were considered tools that allowed information to be shared among members of a community, and therefore contributed to the emergence of nations. As Weber explained,

The degree to which the means of communication have been developed is a condition of decisive importance for the possibility of bureaucratic administration, although it is not the only decisive condition. (Weber 1946, 213)

and later,

[interlocal traffic of mass goods] is among the causal factors in the formation of the modern state. (pp. 213-14)

In this statement, Weber was implicitly referring not only to material goods but also to information goods.

## Communication, Information, and Rising Nationalism

Early theoretical models tend to particularly emphasize the influence that information flows can have on the emergence of nationalities and macropolitical systems. This was the main aspect retained by the social theorists who attempted to quantify the process of diffusion of information technologies.

The early attempts to quantitatively define the role of information within social settings were aimed at proving that an expansion in the communications flow within a given region was accompanied by rising nationalism.

The first studies analyzed aggregate data of communications flows considered as a measure of community integration.[5] These analyses were correlational in nature, and—while valuable in providing the first empirical insights on the developmental models—they did not explain by what mechanisms communication flows contributed to community integration.

Karl Deutsch was the first author to explicitly introduce the notion of information in the analysis of social systems:

There can be no society, no division of labor, without a minimum transfer of information, without communication. (Deutsch 1957, 95)[6]

This statement—as such—did not constitute a theoretical innovation. As shown above, Max Weber had already pointed out the importance of communications and transportation for state-building. Deutsch's merit was that of operationalizing the variable "information" as measurable, and using it to indicate the degrees of community integration. This was done by introducing two concepts: capacity of a communications system, and complementarity of its parts.

Complementarity of two parts of a physical or social system can be measured by the extent to which an operation performed on one of them is transmitted to the other, and by the range of different operations so transmitted. (p. 284)

In that sense, testing complementarity in social settings meant evaluating their communicative effectiveness:

How fast and how accurately do messages get through? How complex and voluminous is the information that can be so transmitted? How effectively are operations on one part of the network transmitted to another? (p. 96)

Having defined this new concept, Deutsch tied it into the notions of people and society by saying that

Membership in a people essentially consists in the ability to communicate more effectively, and over a wider range of subjects, with members of one large group than with outsiders. (p. 97)

Thus, the boundary of a system can be conceived as a line across which interactions are relatively rare and weak compared with those within it (Pool 1973). Deutsch (1957) used this concept to explain the process of nation-building and political integration. Political integration was defined as the existence of a relationship of community among people within the same political entity. He explained that political integration and nation-building occurs when there is a combination of two processes, which he called "mobilization" and "assimilation."

The mobilization process is that which "mobilized individuals for more intensive communication" (Deutsch 1957, 126). Among mobilizing forces, he mentions urbanization, the growth of nonagricultural occupations, the increased usage of information technologies (both media and point-to-point), the growth of the state as a fiscal and military autonomous entity, education, and increased political participation:

There is much evidence to suggest that susceptibility to nationalism increases sharply with social mobilization, that is, with the shift of people away from a subsistence economy and local isolation into exposure to the demonstration effects of more modern technology and practices, to exposure to mass media of communication, to the use of money, to trading with relative strangers, to greater dependence on distant markets, and eventually to literacy, non-agricultural occupations, wage labor, urban residence, membership interest groups or organizations, voting, and other forms of political participation. (Deutsch 1957, 209)

The assimilation process involves not only the learning of language, but also of many cultural habits that are not needed for economic reasons. To put it in Toennies' and Weber's terms, "we may say that assimilation is gaining ground if, in a given territory, community is growing faster than society" (Deutsch, 1957, 125).[7] Among the factors that may exert an influence in the process of political integration and nation-building, Deutsch studied—in particular—the transactions or interactions among persons or groups. The assumption underlying his research was that cohesiveness among individuals and among communities of individuals can be measured by the extent of mutual relationship of interaction among them (Jacob and Teune 1964).

Three types of transactions were studied by Deutsch and other researchers working within the same theoretical framework: (1) communications—the exchange of mail and telephone messages (Deutsch 1956; Taborsky 1960; Deutsch and Isard 1961); (2) trade—the exchange of goods and services (Russett 1963); and (3) mobility (Deutsch 1957). Using transaction flows as quantitative indicators, these researchers developed operational indexes of political cohesion and social change. For example, Deutsch stated that

Between 1945 and 1948 domestic mail rates [in Madagascar] soared; 1948 was the year of extensive nationalistic uprisings in Madagascar. This does not mean that people rise in revolution whenever they write a lot of letters. It does mean that citizens who produce a large volume of letters and who communicate with each other in a fairly intense manner may require different forms of political treatment and administrative attention than a similar population at the low levels of communication of ten or twenty years ago. (Deutsch 1964, 77)

Deutsch also studied the ratio of foreign to domestic mail (Deutsch 1956). He found that the worldwide domestic to foreign mail ratio—which declined from 1880 to 1913, but has been climbing from 1913 on—correlates well with data available on trade and the emergence of national isolationism:

If communication—that is the flow of messages—within the smaller group is much more frequent and much more relevant than is communication across its boundaries, many of the messages will become part of the communication code within the group. The group, that is to say, will develop its own dialect, or its own language, or ideology, or code of measurements, different from the corresponding codes of other groups outside it. (Deutsch 1967, 213)

For measuring the process of nation-building, Deutsch also studied the percentage of total population of given territories that was mobilized and/or assimilated. The underlying hypothesis was that nation-building is the result of a gradual increase in the process of social mobilization—which, in turn, is determined by factors such as urbanization, growth of nonagricultural occupations, information flows, and growth of the state, education, and political participation—all acting in concert. According to this hypothesis, a strong correlation should exist among the measurable indicators of mobilization.

### Introduction of the Economic Variable

In the mid-1970s, the research tradition that analyzed the relationship between communications systems and sociopolitical change gave way to one that focused on the influence of information and communications on economic growth. Models that were developed within this school of thought did not fully consider the political variable, thus giving a partial vision of the interaction of communications and the diverse variables that integrate the process of economic development and social change. Since the early 1960s, microeconomic and macroeconomic theory have pursued research efforts in view of defining the relationship between information/communication and economic systems. The field of information economics has been concerned with

the behavior of [economic] agents who face a situation of uncertainty and engage in information seeking, communicating or processing activity in order to reduce this uncertainty. (Jonscher 1982a, 1)

Within this research body, information was studied as a dependent variable in models explaining price searching (Stigler 1961; Telser 1973), purchasing under quality uncertainty (Akerlof 1970), the behavior of insurance policy markets (Arrow 1963), financial markets (Garbade and Silber 1978), and labor market signaling (Alchian 1969; Gronau 1971).

Despite the number of areas covered, information economic models developed within the 1960s and 1970s generally tended to concentrate on a very specific aspect of economic behavior. The notion of economic uncertainty was only applied to very limited aspects of the functioning of markets—excluding all production processes. And as Jonscher said,

Of the fifty percent or so of the labor effect in the United States economy which is attributable to information handling functions, only a very small proportion can be attributed to price searching, establishing the quality of potential employees or estimating the risk associated within a financial contract. (Jonscher 1982a, 8)

In fact, while economists from Stigler to Arrow have been studying the role of information in microeconomic models, until recently they have displayed little interest in the relationship between information and economic growth. Research on the link between information and economic development was initially performed by communications researchers. Their basic assumption was that "the availability, use, and efficiency of communication goods and services were seen to have a necessary role in national development" (Middleton and Jussawalla 1981, xii). Contributions in the field—which initially started with Lerner (1958) and McClelland (1961)—were more of a sociological than economic nature, even though their implications also had an economic character. According to these authors—as well as Schramm (1964) and Pool (1963)—mass media can have a powerful characterological impact on individuals in a developing society—leading them to become active contributors to the process of modernization and economic growth.

Study of the influence of telecommunication technologies on economic development was performed almost in parallel with—and practically in isolation from—the research on mass media systems. During the 1960s, telecommunications were almost completely overlooked in the literature on communications and development. Works by Lerner (1958) and Schramm (1964) focused exclusively on mass communications. All theoretical approaches to the issue of communications in developing societies emphasized a combination of mass-to-point and interpersonal communications—and the latter, through face-to-face contact rather than through telecommunications (Rogers and Shoemaker 1971).[8]

In the late 1960s, a new approach to the study of social and economic impact of telecommunications started. Most of the studies developed within this approach were performed to support national planning and investment decisions in telecommunications within developing countries. The objective was to demonstrate and quantitatively estimate "the economic value of telecommunications investment" (Saunders, Warford, and Wellenius 1983).

The argument underlying these studies was that

telecommunications infrastructure may be viewed as an input to a productive process, a "factor of production" like petroleum or electricity. (Saunders, Warford, and Wellenius 1983, 73)

In an excellent review of the literature on the topic, Saunders, Warford, and Wellenius (1983) point out that economic benefits to be derived from telecommunications can be of the following types:

1. Telecommunications can substitute cost-effectively for mail usage and personal travel;
2. The telecommunications infrastructure has the potential for increasing productivity "through better management in both the private and public sectors" (p. 14);
3. "Markets gain in effectiveness with improved communication, more rapid responses to market signals become possible, and access to market information is extended at village, town, city, regional, national, and worldwide level" (p. 14).

It is inconceivable that benefits derived from telecommunications investment might have been so clearly spelled out from the starting point of this research tradition. While Lerner's model provided paradigmatic guidance for communications researchers for more than 20 years, research on the impact of telecommunications in the economy was carried out in a more exploratory fashion—without theoretical guidance—but progressively linking itself to more solid theoretical models such as those provided by the information economics tradition.

In a broad sense—and according to the evidence generated within this research tradition—the supply and demand of information technologies are related to the technical and economic progress of a country (Jipp 1963; CCITT 1972; Schapiro 1976; Marsch 1976; Montmaneix 1974; Bebee and Gilling 1976; Hardy 1980; Pierce and Jequier 1982; Jonscher 1981). This basic conclusion does not state much, however, as to the conditions under which this relationship exists. Moreover, since most of the research was produced by economists, it is important to point out the absence of reference to any political variable, which might affect either the relationship between information and economic systems or the process of diffusion of information technologies.

### The Importance of Politics in
### Diffusion of Information Technologies

More than other researchers, communication researchers seem to have been aware of the role of politics in diffusion processes. In his article "Towards a Communication Theory of Modernization," Lerner stated that "one major condition for mass media spread [is] the level of economic development" (1963, 335). Later, he stated that "the general rule is that mass media spread is a direct and monotonic relationship with a rising level of industrial capacity" (p. 336). Further on, however, Lerner stated that, in presenting the principle defined above, he was referring to "the market economy model of the modern Western nations." He considered that

The Soviet system provides some especially interesting deviations from the rule of supply and demand, e.g., the political rule of enforced supply and acquiescent demand for a social commodity taken out of the economic market place. (Lerner 1963, 336)

It is argued here, however, that what Lerner presented as a deviation from the "market economy" model—countries in which media supply is determined by political will—has become a model applicable to Western and developing countries.

In the same conference where Lerner presented his paper, Pool (1963) observed that communist and noncommunist countries have distinctly different approaches when it comes to investing in communications. This has resulted in different communication system structures. Indeed, Pool added that the first policy issue that most emerging nations must resolve is how much of their scarce resources to invest in mass media. Thus, the ranking of investment motives in mass communications becomes a political allocation issue for governments, a matter of national communications policy.

This factor—jointly with industrial policy considerations that affect the development of an information industry—has become a variable as important as the economic one for explaining mass media growth and information technologies' diffusion in general—not only in the developing world, but also in industrialized nations. Which information technology is adopted by a given country is determined in large part by existing patterns of power, influence, and resource allocation in each of the adopting polities. This is why—despite the existence of certain elements of competition—the international market of information technologies is far from being efficient. This seems to be consistent with Apter's (1965) statement that it is important to consider the political rather than the economic variable as being independent in modernizing societies.

The following cases provide some insights on the importance of the political factor in the process of mass media spread. For example, the adoption of a new technology by a given country will constitute a significant incentive for the adoption of the same technology by its neighbors (the "copy your neighbor" principle). Indeed, the installation of a TV station in a frontier zone of a country will foster the installation of a similar station in the border country (the "diffusion by retaliation" principle).

Other political reasons that may push for diffusion of information technologies are of a domestic nature. A government may be compelled to adopt a given communications technology in order to respond to domestic pressures, such as changes in the social and political structure. It might do so because it believes such a response will make it more adaptive, or more efficient, or more able to respond to what the citizens want.

Given the influence of these and other political factors, the concept of market demand as an explanatory variable of international diffusion of a technology (Wells 1972) is substantially affected by political factors. Sometimes governments control the decisional process with regard to communications so thoroughly that mass demand for the medium is reduced by deliberate choice (Frey 1973).

Furthermore, there are some cases in which demand for the medium does not act at all, as a determining factor. For example, in developing countries, the establishment of rural telecommunications does not necessarily reflect the expressed need of users (Jussawalla 1980). In this case, adoption of new technologies may not be related to the advantages of direct users, but in terms of greater centralization—and thus either societal progress, political control, or both.

Telecommunications, postal, and computer diffusion studies in developing countries have focused—almost exclusively—on the economic variable. Research has usually focused on the relationship between two variables: the extent of telephone provision and the level of economic development. With the exception of a few media studies (Cutright 1963; Lerner 1958)—no attention has been given to the influence of the political factor in the process of technological diffusion. In addition, whenever a study analyzed the interaction between media and political development, the term "political development" has been defined in terms of increased participation—never in terms of the expansion of state intervention in civil society.

A phenomenon as pervasive as the expansion of government has to necessarily have an impact on the diffusion of information technologies. While demand for telecommunications and computing emerge—in last instance—from the social fabric, in many cases the state can control its supply. In reviewing the literature on diffusion of information technologies, very few references have been found to the demand for technologies emerging from the political apparatus. References to political and economic factors acting in concert to determine diffusion of information technologies has become more common only in recent years. For example, Snow explains that different countries, administrations and operating entities are able to select [telecommunications technologies] based on a combination of economic, political, and perhaps sociological factors.... The choice is made within a framework of optimization subject to constraints imposed by the technology, resource scarcities, market imperfections and institutional factors. (Snow 1986, 6)

Despite the recent identification of the political variable as a key in determining diffusion of information technologies, its influence is only implicitly introduced in most of the models presented in the scholarly literature. For example, a model developed to explain growth in mail traffic (UPU 1971) includes two independent variables (post tariffs and telephone rates) that are clearly set by political decision and are motivated by policy imperatives. Another example of influence of the political system on information technology diffusion is the policy control on diffusion of telecommunication technologies. While telecommunications demand can be ultimately linked to economic development, the expansion of the telecommunications infrastructure in most countries of the world is a decision that pertains to the political authorities. Attali and Stourdze (1977) and Perry (1977) have shown how government policies retarded telephone growth in the cases of France and England, respectively. Moreover, the growth of mass media systems is also strongly linked to regulatory decisions, such as those that allocate the frequency spectrum to potential suppliers of programs.

Diffusion of telecommunications technology is strongly determined by government policy, with the possible exception of loosely regulated technologies—such as citizen band radio—that could be better explained by a mix of policy factors and market demand. Diffusion of computer technology is less determined by government policy and more related to domestic structure of demand. However, certain economic policies—such as import substitution—may affect equipment pricing, and, as a result, delay the computerization of local firms.

The role of governments in the process of diffusion of information technologies was also recently spelled out by Jonscher:

Improvements [in information labor productivity] may not be realized without active intervention by governments and other policy makers.... There are many steps between the availability of a higher performance chip and the achievement of more efficient information management in the economy as a whole. (Jonscher 1983, 27)[9]

Why are governments interested in controlling the diffusion of information technologies? Reasons can range from industrial policy considerations to the need of restricting free flow of information within the citizenry. Many political scientists see information technologies as an important element for exercising power and control over populations and territories. Information technologies have been variously named the "nerves" (Deutsch 1963), "blood," or "skeleton" of the political system. According to Frey (1973), the perceived functions of communications within the political system can be linked to at least two aspects:

1. the provision of information for more effective instrumental decision making; and
2. the increase of power and control. This focuses on communications and information for integration as needed by the new differentiation, specialization, and heightened collective aspirations, and on communication for responsiveness by power holders.

In sum, we believe that diffusion of information technologies is determined by the interaction of a plurality of variables, among which the economy plays an important—but not exclusive—role. The diffusion of an information technology is determined by the interaction between several factors, among which the configuration of the technology, its economics, and its political desirability are key. While the communications literature has conceptually accounted for the importance of political factors, little has been done in terms of using both economic and political variables for explaining communications systems growth. There is an urgent need to globally account for these factors in the research performed in the future. A model that incorporates both economic and political variables within a comprehensive framework is needed to explain diffusion of information technologies. In the next section, we propose an overall comprehensive framework of causality, including both economic and political variables.

## STRUCTURAL CAUSALITY AND DIFFUSION OF INFORMATION TECHNOLOGIES

As discussed in the introduction of this chapter, while correlation exists between economic development and expansion of information technologies infrastructure, some of the relationships between the economic system and the information and communications systems are mediated by the political system. In addition, diffusion of information technologies can also be exclusively the result of needs emerging from the political system—having little to do with market mechanisms. In this case, the political variable is considered "an exogenous variable affecting communications development" (Duch and Lemieux 1986). In a framework of causal inferences, this set of relationships can be plotted as follows:

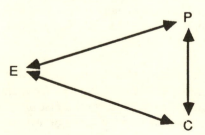

in which: E measures economic growth; P measures needs emerging from the political system; and C indicates the expansion of the communications and information infrastructure.

According to this model, communications development and diffusion of information technologies are linked to the process of overall political-economic development by means of reciprocal interactions within an ecological context. The model places the communications variable in a structural system of causality within which the economic and/or political factors can have an influence on its development.

Having defined the general model, it is important to accurately define each of the variables included in it. What makes this task particularly complex is the fact that each of the variables can have a different significance, and may measure different phenomena. For example, the concept of "political system" can either mean the state apparatus or the political environment. Similarly the "economic factor" can refer to aggregate consumer demand or production processes. Finally, the category "information technologies" includes such different technologies as radio and computers.

Nevertheless, this model constitutes a good starting point in developing a new framework for understanding the relationship among economics, politics, and communications. Any attempt at quantification will have to be based on the disaggregation and conceptualization of each of these three variables.

Despite the generalization implicit in the model, it has several advantages. First, it reintroduces the political variable, which has been completely ignored in recent research efforts. Second, a structural system of causality provides the opportunity to analyze new relationships in and among the political, the economic, and the technological levels within a new structured whole (Slack 1984). Third, the inclusion of both the economic and the political variables within a structural causality framework enables us to consider the historical specificity of different models—such as Lerner's (1963)—which precisely represent a particular case of the relationship between information technologies and society. According to this notion, the hierarchy of causality, and the weight (or importance) of each independent variable will be specific to each historical epoch. In that sense, the model analyzes information technologies within a particular "historically constituted social whole" and explains the relationships between information technologies "and the whole as it changes" (Slack 1984, 90).

Finally, this approach rejects the notion that information technologies are ultimate determinants of political and economic development. On the contrary, it provides a structural framework of causality in which information technologies are conceived as one of many determinants in the development and survival of political and economic systems.

Having defined in broad terms the framework of structural causality that includes political, economic, and informational variables, we will now focus on the different ways these variables can relate to one another. In the first place, the communications and information variable—measured in terms of level of diffusion of information technologies—may react to specific needs arising from the political system. The term "political system" in this case includes "the entire scope of political activities within a society" (Almond and Powell 1978), but addresses in particular the state apparatus.

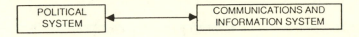

The causality link is bi-directional because, in meeting the needs emerging from the political system, a communications system influences whatever political developments to which it is reacting.

In the second place, there is the articulation of needs emerging from the economic system—which are directly satisfied by the communications and information system.

As in the previous case, the two variables are linked by bi-directional causality. This relationship has been proved in a wealth of studies.

Finally, although the communications and information system may react to needs emerging from the economy the relationship between the two variables is mediated by the political system—in particular, the policymaking process.

This is a particular case of the relationship depicted above. Its importance resides on the fact that the political system may sometimes act as an obstacle to the satisfaction of informational needs emerging from the economy.

The decomposition of the structural causality framework in these three cases has been done exclusively for analytical purposes. In the real world, the communication system often reacts simultaneously to needs emerging from both the economic and the political systems. For example, Innis—in his empirical study of the Canadian Pacific Railway (Innis 1923)—showed how the expansion of Canada toward the west was influenced by an extension of the transportation and communication system to meet economic and political objectives. The author explained that

Physical expansion of the [Canadian Pacific Railway] to a large extent determined, and was determined by, the growth of traffic. . . . *The addition of technical equipment described as physical property of the Canadian Pacific Railway Company was a cause and an effect of the strength and character of [Western] civilization....* [In French Canada] the seigneurial system, the effects of military struggle, the character of [the] St. Lawrence River Basin, the influences of language, religion and customs promoted the development of homogeneous settlement, and the growth of a distinct national feeling. (Innis, as quoted by I. Parker 1981, 134, emphasis added by the author)

According to Innis, a transportation technology (which could be likened to any communications technology) constitutes a key factor in determining "structures of spatial-temporal relations" within a social system. At the same time, its character and deployment is determined by the social, economic, and political foundations of such systems. Innis's case study shows how development of a transportation technology serves not only economic but also political needs.

In addition to building a structural causality model that avoids any technological determinisms, Innis emphasized the importance of the political variable in determining the emergence and deployment of information technologies. In his later work on empires, Innis shows how the extension of the power of empires depended on effective systems of communication. From a historical perspective, changes in the technology of communication allowed for changes in the possibilities for the extension of political entities.

Contemporary commentators of Innis's work have emphasized the importance of this concept. For example, Heyer explained how, in Innis's research,

the media of communication do not constitute a causal nexus but are an integral element in the way holistically distinct realities arise out of former ones. (Heyer 1981, 256–57)

Similarly, I. Parker (1981) stated that communications and information activities are carried out within social systems at both their economic and political levels. Parker mentioned four basic communication activities that can serve both economic and political functions: (1) transportation and storage of material goods and commodities, (2) transportation of persons, (3) transmission of "property claims to real resources" through monetary transfers, and (4) transmission of information.

There is another dimension that needs to be addressed when considering this causality model: that of international relations. In describing the structural causality framework, we have only drawn examples of endogenous relationships existing within a single system. Yet, the communications system within a region or country can react to external political and/or economic factors. For example, if we consider the first causal relationship linking communications and information to politics, we can find cases in which the information technology infrastructure of a given country may react to needs emerging from a country's competitive situation in the world system. If, as Skocpol argues, nation-states are...organizations geared to maintain control of home territories and populations and *to undertake actual or potential military competition with other states in the international system* (Skocpol 1979, 22, emphasis added by the author)[10]

then it is logical to conceive that some of the developments occurring in the communications system are a reaction to the moves of other polities within the international system. As the same author stated,

Recurrent warfare within the system of states prompted European monarchs and statesmen *to centralize, regiment, and technologically upgrade armies and fiscal administrations.* (p. 21, emphasis added by the author)

Both actions of centralizing and technologically upgrading the military and the bureaucracy are supported by information technologies, especially at the level of information transfer and record keeping. Thus, Skocpol implicitly provides an example in which developments in communications may occur as a result of political developments in the international arena.

It can also be the case that economic developments in systems external to a nation-state can affect internal communications development. Again, following Skocpol,

As capitalism has spread across the globe, transnational flows of trade and investment have affected all countries.... Moreover, as "peripheral" areas of the globe were incorporated into world economic networks centered on the more industrially advanced countries, their pre-existing economic [author's note: and communication] structures and class relations were often reinforced or modified in ways inimical to subsequent self-sustaining and diversified growth. (p. 20)

Thus, it is logical that, in some cases, communications development may occur as a way to meet needs emerging from other economies, in order to facilitate the articulation of peripheral areas into an international network of interdependence.

The articulation of cross-system relationships between the three variables can be graphically represented as shown in Figure 3.1. The communications infrastructure of system B (country B) can react to exogenous influences originated in system A (country A).

In summary: First, we identified a structural causality framework that links the economic, political, and informational/communicational variables within a set of mutual relationships. Second, we analyzed each of these relationships. Third, we included an international political and economic dimension to the aforementioned relationships. A historical dimension will now be considered.

As expressed above, this model of structural causality operates in different ways according to each historical epoch. The hierarchy of causality—or, as expressed in statistical terms, the weight of each of the independent variables— will vary historically. According to theories of political and economic development, nations generally go through a three-phase process. The first phase, which

**Figure 3.1**
**Structural Causality at the International Level**

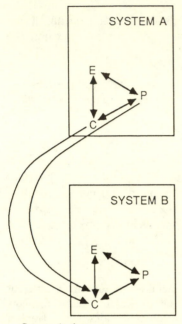

*Source:* Author.

could be labeled "state-building," is characterized by the formation of a political and institutional framework aimed at supporting political control and economic growth. The objectives are twofold:

1. the formation or restructuring of a bureaucratic administration in the Weberian sense, with clearly defined roles at a judicial, financial, and administrative level; and

2. the development of a military force capable of institutionalizing and externalizing the authority of the state.

In this first stage of state-building, information technologies are mainly used by the state apparatus. Thus, the political variable has more weight than the economic variable in determining their diffusion. The only force capable of obtaining resources necessary for expanding its information technologies infrastructure is the state. These resources are drawn from the population and territory that it controls.

The second phase, which we might call "infrastructure building for economic development," is when the state emphasizes the buildup of material infrastructures aimed at supporting economic growth. In this phase, communications development is driven by economic needs, mediated by the political system.

The third phase—that of "maturity"—is when the investment by the state in infrastructure stagnates; defense and administration are then the only activities in the government sector that foster diffusion of information technologies. However, as a result of the industrialization process, the manufacturing and service sectors become the main contributors to the expansion of information and communication systems. In this phase, the economic variable is the one that has more weight in determining communications development.

This typical process tends to vary from country to country. While industrialized countries have followed the three stages in a more or less linear fashion, developing countries tend to face the challenges of stage-building and economic development simultaneously. It is precisely the simultaneity of the economic and political development processes in developing countries that sometimes tends to hide the importance of the political variable in explaining the expansion of the communications and information infrastructure.

Having exposed—in very general terms—a historical model that shows the influence of the political variable on communications and information development, we will now concentrate on analyzing the mechanisms by which this influence is enacted. According to our historical model, the first phase of state-building is dominated by the political system, which is the key driver in the diffusion of information technologies. This process is analyzed in the next section. Following this, we focus on analyzing the impact of industrial policies, a case in which the state acts as a mediator of needs emerging from the economic structure. Finally, we analyze how private sector demand becomes the main driver of communication and information systems growth. This section also discusses the future prospects for state intervention in the information technology field in developing countries.

## INFORMATION TECHNOLOGIES DIFFUSION
## AS DRIVEN BY THE PROCESS OF STATE BUILDING

The existence of the state as a political entity results from a formative process through which the institution gradually acquires a set of attributes that show a distinct level of political development. Nettl (1968) considered that the state must develop two properties: (1) the material capacities to control, extract, and allocate societal resources within a given population and territory; and (2) the symbolic capacities to create and diffuse collective identities and loyalties among the citizens of a nation. In a similar vein, Schmitter et al. (1979) have defined several attributes of the state—namely, its capacity to: (1) externalize its power; (2) institutionalize its authority; (3) differentiate its control; and (4) internalize a collective identity.

The first attributed defined by Schmitter et al. is linked to the recognition of the state as a sovereign entity within the international political system. The second implies the imposition of a power structure capable of exercising a monopoly over the organized means of coercion. The third attribute implies the emergence of functionally differentiated public institutions that are relatively autonomous with respect to civil society. They must have a recognized capacity to extract, on a regular basis, resources from society; a certain degree of professionalization of their functionaries in the Weberian sense; and a certain measure of centralized control over their multiple activities. The fourth attribute is the power of the state to generate symbols that reinforce social cohesion.

The process of developing this set of attributes leads to the emergence of a political center, which progressively controls and hegemonizes a periphery—conceived as the national space. The political center is "the gathering place where the major decisions are made" (Rokkan 1973), while the periphery is constituted by the territorial populations dependent on the decisions made at such centers.[11] The notion of center can have several dimensions—such as political, historical, economic, or linguistic. Accordingly, a national territory can have several centers: One could be the political capital (the site of the central government); another, the major economic and financial center; and several others, equally important linguistic centers.

Peripheries are always dependent on the existence of a center. As Gottman stated,

In geographical terms, the periphery is what surrounds the centre, a geometrical relationship; the farther away a point is from the centre, the more peripheral it would be. But the political relationship is different: peripheral location means subordination to the centre. (Gottman 1980, 16)

The notions of political centrality and control of the periphery by the center are closely related to the concept of communication system. In fact, the initial formulation of the idea of centrality assumed certain conditions with regard to the communications system surrounding the center. In the first reference to the idea of center–periphery, Von Thuenen (original 1826; English version 1966) expressed it this way:

Imagine a very large town at the centre of a fertile plain, which is crossed by no navigable river or canal. (as quoted by Gottman 1980, 16)

Von Thuenen's simplified model assumed political, economic, and geographical centrality, as well as uniform conditions of transportation and communication.

The relevance of the notion of communication system to the understanding of the concept of political centrality is based on the fact that the dominance of the periphery by the center can be determined by studying the transactions between center and periphery. The volume and variety of transactions is conditioned by objective factors, such as the physical conditions of transportation and communication. The technology of communications and transportation also determine the potential reach of efforts of political and economic expansion (Deutsch 1957; 1963).

Rokkan (1980) depicted the process of state-building as three parallel processes of penetration of the periphery by means of increasingly complex systems of communication and control: military-administrative; economic; and cultural. Rokkan explained that

for each of these processes of territorial aggregation, the model posits a distinctive set of centralized agencies. These need not control separate physical locations, but may in some cases be found together in close fusion in one dominant center. (Rokkan 1980, 165)

Resistance against this centralizing drive may appear if

there is some basis of independent economic growth within the periphery and the cultural authorities find it increasingly difficult to satisfy the demands for subsidies, transfers, and the like made on them by the leaders of the periphery (p. 199)

and/or if

few ties of communication, alliance and bargaining experience towards the national center and more towards external centers of cultural or economic influence [appear]. (p. 121)

If communication processes are so important to the notion of political centrality, it is necessary to consider information technologies as a key factor in the process of state-building.

Analyzing the use of information technologies by a political center engaged in penetrating and hegemonizing its periphery, Strassoldo argued that

coercive power, based on continuous surveillance by the dominant of the subordinate's behavior and on quick deployment of threats and punishments, is clearly tied to material conditions such as efficient communication lines and distribution of coercive "resources" on the dominated territory. (Strassoldo 1980, 38)

Similarly, Deutsch—in his pioneering work on nationalism and social communication—defined a center in terms of nodal areas of intense social communication, which dominate wide surrounding areas "in terms of transportation, strategies and economics" (Deutsch 1957, 39).

Within Deutsch's framework, power is defined as control over communication flows, and such control is put into practice at the nodes of the channel systems. The cybernetic approach to the study of political systems has a certain overlap to the center–periphery approach, particularly in its organismic aspects (Strassoldo 1980). The polity is composed by a nucleus and a territory, and decisions made at the nucleus or center affect the whole system.

Research within the cybernetic tradition—such as Deutsch's—tried to measure the political performance of states against the global intensity of their information flows. However, while establishing a relationship between nation-building and information flows, the first studies did not provide any clues as to how—by what mechanisms—information flows improved state performance. This is due to the fact that the notion of state was almost completely ignored by the cybernetic tradition.

In an effort to reintroduce the idea of state, we argue that the transmission of messages across an extended territory leads to the creation of networks of specialized political relations. Historically, the organizational response of political systems engaged in the process of penetration of their peripheries was to differentiate the distribution of roles within their bureaucracies. In formal systems—where a center is penetrating a periphery—progressive centralization is "the consequence of progressive segregation (i.e., internal differentiation) of systems" (Strassoldo 1980, 41). The longer the lines of command and communication within the system, the more differentiated the distribution of roles (Rokkan 1973). For example, the differentiation of military organizations (armies and police) allowed the control of new territories. Communications and information played a key role within this process of differentiation aimed at controlling the national territory. As Innis (1950) argued, empires depended on some form of cultural standardization through the medium of script, for transmission of information within the networks of control.

Communication technologies—from script to computers and telecommunications—have the potential for reducing range and scope of cross-territorial communications. Information technologies have a direct impact on flows at three levels: speed of transmission, volumes, and range (Claval 1980; Deutsch 1957; Wiener 1948). As a result, information technologies play a substantial role in the process of development of state attributes.

This role has been thoroughly studied in the case of the relation of mass media and national cohesion (Pye 1963; Pool 1963; Deutsch 1957; Schramm 1964; Frey 1973). For example, in two case studies of development communications projects, Clippinger (1976) found that governments were the principal beneficiaries of the projects. In his study of satellite communications in Algeria and educational television in El Salvador, the author found that, in both cases, the usage of communications technology resulted in greater concentration of power within the government, and reduction or diffusion of power for those outside the government:

In El Salvador the government, through the Ministry of Education, extended its influence over teachers and students without appreciably increasing the number of students employed. In Algeria, telecommunications development has enhanced the government position and furthered the influence and dominance of the urban industrialized areas in Algerian affairs, without any apparent positive effect on the rural and traditional sectors. (Clippinger 1976)

Clippinger linked the use of information technologies by the government to the transitional nature of the economic, political, and cultural institutions of both developing countries.

The interaction between information technologies and the monopoly over organized means of coercion was recognized as far back as two centuries ago. Attali and Stourdze quote C. Chappe, the inventor of the visual telegraph, who said:

The day will come when the government will be able to achieve the grandest idea we can possibly have of power, by using the telegraph system in order to spread directly, every day, every hour, and simultaneously, its influence over the whole republic. (Attali and Stourdze 1977, p. 97)

Information technologies can help not only transmitting, but also processing and storing information needed by the state to achieve its control over the national territory. Using Hirschman's (1970) terms, telecommunications give the population of a given country the possibility for using its "voice" within the internal system, but it can also create walls against cultural "exits" into other territories.

Finally, information technology is necessarily linked to the third state attribute: extracting resources from society and managing the *res publica*. A high percentage of the computers in developing countries are used by the government for public administration purposes. For example, the public sector in Mexico represents the largest consumer of a wide variety of information products: It

**Figure 3.2**
**National Expenditures in Data Processing, Mexico**

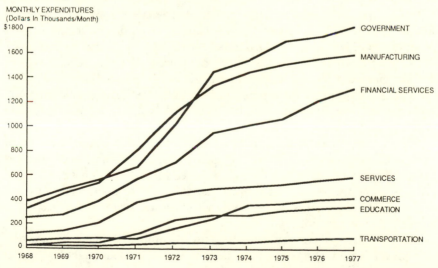

*Source: Diagnostic on Informatics in Mexico.* Secretariat of Budget and Planning, Mexico, 1980, p. 103.

Table 3.1
National Expenditures in Data Processing, Brazil

|  | 1975 | | 1976 | |
|---|---|---|---|---|
|  | U.S. Dollars | Share | U.S. Dollars | Share |
| Public Sector | 2,481,065 | (39.6%) | 4,424,733 | (42.4%) |
| Private Sector | 3,773,590 | (60.3%) | 6,008,710 | (57.5%) |
| Total | 6,254,655 | (100.0%) | 10,433,443 | (100.0%) |

Source: Recursos Computacionais Brasileiros. CAPRE, 1977, p. 29.

represents a little more than 29 percent of the total domestic consumption of computers and related equipment. Furthermore, until 1977 the growth rate of computing capacity of the Mexican government was higher than that of the manufacturing sector and similar to that of the financial sector as the slope of both curves in Figure 3.2 indicate.

Statistics for Brazil show that, in 1976, the public sector spent 42 percent of the national expenditure in data processing (see Table 3.1).

However, one should not overemphasize the role of information technologies in the process of state-building. Paraphrasing Innis, the use of script alone does not determine the emergence of empires. If the transmission speed and capacity of lines remain slow, the state apparatus remains limited in its efficiency, but continues to exist.

In fact, the administrative organization of the state apparatus is the main factor, when exercising control. Claval called it, "a particular organization of space, i.e., its division into limited areas where supervision can be exercised" (1980, p. 66). This is the basis on which a bureaucracy is built: Individuals loyal to the center are located at the transmission and observations points. The physical organization of the national territory and the utilization of information technologies determine the speed at which orders are transmitted from the center to the periphery.

We have reviewed the importance of information technologies on historical state-building processes. It is worth considering the impact of new communications and information technologies on the need for a central physical point of political authority. Multicenter polities may develop, especially when telecommunications allow control centers to be not in central locations with respect to communication networks.

It would seem—then—that, with the cost of communications and information processing dropping, the center–periphery arrangement might lose its political validity. However, as Deutsch (1963) explained, political systems strive for concentration of control, not necessarily of things and people. Developing countries do not seem to be engaged in this type of decentralizing path. In most cases the political system is engaged in physical centralization processes. The lack of resources to invest in geographically decentralizing technologies prevents less developed countries (LDCs) from developing the peripheries. Centralization seems to be the general political development pattern, unless demands arising from the periphery pose a disintegrative threat to the whole polity. In that case, the state will tend to decentralize by various means, including deployment of information technologies.

## THE IMPACT OF INDUSTRIAL POLICIES

Beyond the first stage of state-building, the expansion of the state generally leads to the buildup of an information infrastructure aimed not only at optimizing the functioning of bureaucratic structures, but also at better serving the new needs emerging from the economic system. The buildup of an information infrastructure appears as a logical consequence of the expanding role of the state in the economy.

This process has an influence on the diffusion of information technologies at three levels. First, due to the increased role of the state in administrating and regulating the economic system, information technologies are needed to improve government efficiency in controlling, extracting, and allocating societal resources with regard to the population and the territory (Nettl 1968). Second, the process of redistribution of state expenditures leads to increased investment in areas such as environmental and social services, which are heavily supported by information technologies. As a result of these two factors, it is natural that the information technologies infrastructure "emerge[s] by and large within the public sphere and under its regulation" (Snow 1986, 7).

A third, conceptually distinct influence on information technology diffusion is when the state promotes industrial policies to foster development of an information industry. Governments may emerge as active drivers for the development of an information industry whose products are purchased in most cases by the domestic market. Examples such as the Brazilian and Indian computer policies and the French telecommunications development plan constitute cases where an industrial policy is a key factor driving supply and, in consequence, diffusion of information technologies.

In many cases, however, diffusion of information technologies is not promoted—but restrained—by government policy. For example, diffusion of the telephone in Europe was in its origins partially affected by political determinants. The diffusion of telecommunications in Europe has been no random or single market-driven process. On the contrary, it has been constrained and/or driven forward through deliberate government policy decisions.

Another example of the influence regulatory policies have on the diffusion of an information technology is the case of the telegraph in some developing countries. The decline of the telegraph in some countries of the developing world seems to be a much slower process than the one experienced in the United States and other market-oriented economies. This situation is generally due to the fact that the government, which controls both the telegraph and the telephone, typically assumes a risk-averting behavior with regard to the introduction of new technology. If the government were to develop a long-distance telephone network that would act as an efficient substitute for the telegraph, the telegraph system would suffer huge losses. Therefore, the slow development of a telephone network in some developing countries—although basically due to lack of capital—has the net effect of protecting the telegraph investment.

Examples of regulatory control of technology diffusion in developed countries are also numerous. In the United States, for example, diffusion of domestic satellites and cable TV was considerably delayed by regulatory mechanisms. In the first case, despite the fact that the first successful communications satellite was launched in 1962, it was not until 1975 that the first U.S. domestic satellite was put in space. In this case, as evidenced in numerous studies (Socol 1977; Irwin 1981), the reason for the delay was the fear that satellites would bypass established telephone trunks, because of cost-effective rates.

Sometimes, the restriction of information technologies diffusion may be the counter-intuitive result of related public policies. In Brazil, for example, the diffusion of computers was restricted both by raising the barriers to entry of foreign firms and by increasing the cost of equipment, as a result of import-substitution policies. The net effect of this measure was the temporary slowing in the country's rate of computerization (Katz 1981). The Brazilian case also proves that governments can not only control the diffusion of technologies they operate, but can also regulate the diffusion of information technologies among private users.

Another well-known case of control over the process of diffusion among private users is the regulation of the electromagnetic spectrum. This is justified on the basis that the number of frequencies is limited and private markets cannot assure their continued availability because individual firms will have a tendency to suboptimize their allocation. No matter whether this analysis is still technically valid or not, the fact is that, in most countries of the world, spectrum allocation control remains an optimal measure for controlling access to the broadcasting market and, in many countries, for preserving either oligopolistic or monopolistic industry structures.

## WILL DEREGULATION OF THE INFORMATION INDUSTRIES EVER OCCUR IN DEVELOPING COUNTRIES?

In parallel to the process in which the state in industrialized countries heavily invested in communications and information infrastructure in order to facilitate economic growth, the private sector underwent structural changes. The increased technical efficiency that resulted from the industrialization process led to increasingly complex production processes.[12]

As a result, the manufacturing sector devised an organizational response (decentralization of production units) and a technological response (adoption of information technologies) in order to render information workers more productive. This marked the passage from the second development phase—in which the state was the main adopter of information technologies—to the third— where the industrial and nongovernmental sector, in general, became the main factor driving diffusion of information technologies. This dynamic is emphasized by Snow when he states that "Pressure for change in regulation— typically, for deregulation—has come by and large from the user community, especially from large multinational business users" (1986, 10).

This phase—which we label "maturity"—is characteristic of certain industrialized countries. In the case of developing countries, the situation is different, since we are dealing with state structures that are still going through their formation processes—with low pressure coming from the private sector for developing and deregulating a communications infrastructure.

Is this state of affairs permanent? What are the major trends with regard to political intervention in the transition to informational stages of development? This chapter has argued that, in all countries, political intervention is the key variable in the first stages of development of an information infrastructure. However, as industrialization progresses, the private sector will take the lead in driving diffusion of information technologies.

The deregulatory process in LDCs is slowed down by economic and political factors. First, in most developing countries, economies of scale and scope still preclude the transition from a public monopolistic telecommunications environment to a competitive one. In the case of mass media, if these have achieved saturation levels in their diffusion, the state is less likely to be able to intervene in controlling media growth (Duch and Lemieux 1986).

Second, regulation or deregulation of information technologies is also determined by historical and politico-ideological factors (Jonscher 1986). Hirschman—in his book *Shifting Involvements* (1982)—has observed that, over time, countries go through major swings in the relative roles they assign to public and private sectors. As described by Paul,

The 1960s, for example, saw a shift in favour of public action in the United States and some European countries. By the mid-1970's, in the same countries, the pendulum had begun to swing in the other direction towards the private sector. In the developing world, the role of the public sector expanded significantly in the 1950's and 1960's. Among other things, this trend may have been a reaction to the dominance of private enterprise in the colonial era. In recent years, we have begun to see a swing back to the private sector in some of these countries. The oscillations in the public-private choice mix of societies seem to be heavily influenced by the gap that emerges between the public's expectations of a sector and their experience. (Paul 1985, 3)

The differences that can be observed between the deregulating trend in the information technology field in developed countries—such as the United

States, the United Kingdom, Japan, and France—and the situation of strict government control in developing countries has to be analyzed against each country's historical experience.

The Latin American experience appropriately illustrates this point. The extraordinary expansion of world trade in the nineteenth century and the availability and internationalization of capital flows opened new opportunities for investment in productive and intermediary activity in Latin America. National governments in most of the Latin American countries had to satisfy the needs of a stable order, and promote conditions that favored economic expansion. However, the governments that were supposed to meet these challenges had a strong dependence on external finance and a serious lack of resources.

These government policies of promoting economic expansion were directed toward the creation of conditions that favored the expansion of an export and mercantile economy. During the final third of the nineteenth century, an initial communications infrastructure (telegraphic and postal systems) was built. In many cases, the initial Latin American communication systems were the result of direct foreign investment—given the lack of locally available capital. Thus, we find that, at the beginning of the twentieth century, many telecommunications utilities were owned by foreign companies.

The nationalistic wave of the 1960s and early 1970s led to the expropriation and consolidation of most telecommunication companies—such as the examples of Chile under the Allende government, and Argentina during the democratic experience of 1973-76. The authoritarian wave that swept Latin America and is currently coming to an end did not necessarily mean the end of nationalistic policies. In fact, in the early 1970s, the Brazilian Navy led the process of policy formulation in the computer field. The idea of the nation as a military unit and of a computer industry as one of the foundations of military power motivated the navy's concern for industrialization. It regarded industrialization as a military strategy that should concentrate on certain specific industries crucially important to the nation's military strength.

This experience was the starting point for renewed interest in information technology policymaking on the part of the Brazilian military, which has tightly controlled a process of accelerated technological innovation ever since. Interestingly enough, the intervention has been limited to areas such as telecommunications and computing.

What effect will the resurgence of democracy in Latin America have on information technology policymaking? The most dynamic area of state intervention will be in protecting key information industries that have been controlled by foreigners, or the subject of foreign interest. Most governments in Latin America assign a strategic value to telecommunications and computing. As a result, industrial policymaking in this area will continue to be an active endeavor— Brazil, Mexico, and Argentina being at the forefront. Government intervention by means of state-owned information industry companies will most likely be excluded. Policies will evolve between, on the one hand, stimulating the development of national companies to compete with and replace the multinational corporations that control the market, and, on the other, cooperating with the multinationals and influencing them so that the country obtains a part of the benefits accruing from their activities.

What will happen to the public agencies supplying telecommunication services? The key factor in this case is the resurgence of democracy itself. This phenomenon will most naturally increase possibilities for the public to express—directly or indirectly—its opinion on the organization and delivery of the services. Democratic public control (Paul 1985) will constitute a pressure toward improvement in the service, and—potentially—to privatization. It is doubtful that Latin American governments will accept privatization—at least in the short run—given that telecommunication public agencies are in general, one of the few state enterprises that are profitable.

What is the situation in Africa? This continent has been strongly influenced both by a reaction to the dominance of private enterprise in the colonial era, as well as by the statist information-technology policies of the former colonial powers. The policies and attitudes of the advanced countries toward the developing nations have an important formative influence on African countries. Advanced countries have provided development assistance in developing countries on a growing scale, as a means of either strengthening the new nations' independence or enlisting their political support. The donors' influence tends to support and reinforce the patterns and specific decisions of economic policy. Some advanced countries—such as France—have placed considerable emphasis on autarchy and on the pursuit of statist policies; they have analyzed the problems of developing countries, and advocated development strategies from this perspective.

Interestingly enough, international modeling influences operate under a time lag: The imitating country may still be implementing certain policies that the model country has already abandoned due to lack of effectiveness. While both France and the United Kingdom are undergoing a process of tightly paced deregulation, African countries are faithfully attached to the old statist model of communications development. In the case of the African countries, the time-lag factor may be operating simultaneously with the still significant role that the public sector has to play in their development. This might introduce an obstacle to technological innovation.

Nevertheless, some African governments have shown pragmatism, in order to keep up with the international pace of information technological innovation. For example, by creating semiprivate monopolies and relinquishing total government control (Katz and Lefevre 1980), a few governments such as Ivory Coast, Senegal, and Kenya have succeeded in speeding up the process of adoption of satellite communications.

Asian countries have also shown pragmatism in their formulation of information technology policies. After years of restricting the computerization of the country, the Indian government is unleashing some of the nation's potential for technological innovation and private sector participation in the manufacturing of data processing equipment (Katz 1984). China also seems to be moving in the same direction, with regard to the diffusion of computing. Both countries are being influenced by the Korean and Taiwanese industrialization and development models.

It should be made clear, however, that a redefinition of the role of the state in the information field will not mean a complete withdrawal of governments from the field of information technology. The trend combines a tendency toward privatization of information goods production and delivery of service, as well as a strict control by the state of variables such as market access, imports, and spectrum allocation.

In conclusion, the state will still play a key role in the transition toward an information society. We are witnessing a redefinition of the state's means of intervention: The main examples are control of market access; regulation of service supply; and industrial policy, in its larger sense.

Will developing countries ever deregulate their information industries—the way some industrialized nations are doing? Even if privatization progresses in the developing world, the chances are that governments will continue to control the main aspects of the diffusion of information technologies, and will therefore attempt to act as intermediaries determining the impact of market variables on their countries' transition paths toward postindustrial stages.

## CONCLUSION

This chapter's main argument is that societies tend to adopt information technologies not only on the basis of technical feasibility or economic profitability, but also in terms of political desirability.

After extensively reviewing the literature on diffusion of information technologies, we concluded that most of the recent theories put forward to explain the interaction between information, communications, and society have focused almost exclusively on economic and social variables—excluding the political ones. Yet, the influence of political factors have been implicit in most of these explanations. In particular, it was pointed out that even a phenomenon as pervasive as the expansion of the state and its influence on the diffusion of information technologies has been only superficially explored.

Based on this finding, a historical model aimed at explaining the causes of diffusion of information technologies was presented. According to this model, diffusion of information technologies is a process contingent on economic, social, and political variables. The importance of each of these variables changes, according to different historical epochs. In the first stage of political development—state-building—it is the political variable that closely controls the diffusion process. For example, new states typically keep a strict control over the diffusion of mass communication technologies—allowing the diffusion of only those that serve the purpose of creating a sense of national identity within societies often composed of disparate ethnic, tribal, or linguistic elements.

Since, at this stage, the political variable is the most important in influencing diffusion of information technologies, the networks of international influence are key in determining the introduction of technologies in a given country.

In the second developmental stage, the economic variable gains weight, and information technologies are needed as part of each country's infrastructure for supporting economic growth. Yet, still at this stage, the political system may act as a constraint on the satisfaction of informational needs emerging from the economy, by means of the regulatory process, or as an impetus for diffusion by means of industrial policy.

In the third developmental stage—maturity—two parallel processes challenge the hegemony of the political variable. In the first place, the private sector becomes the main user of communication and information systems, and tends to develop a conflictive relationship with the regulatory structures of the state. In the second place, technological developments lead to a decrease in the price of equipment. This decrease in the price of message production devices limits the government's capability to enforce the control of diffusion of technologies. Media policies in France and Italy allowing for the installation of private radio stations, and legislation in Mexico authorizing the installation of satellite antennae for receiving television programs from U.S. cable and broadcasting networks are two examples of regulatory frameworks that have been obliged to adapt to challenges coming from the private sector. In conclusion, the stage of maturity is associated with a decline in importance of the political variable, and an increase in relevance of economic factors in determining diffusion of information technologies.

This chapter also identified the mechanisms by which government intervention is enacted. First, regulation can act to control access to the source of supply of media signals—therefore restricting the diffusion of receiving equipment. Second, policymakers can restrict access to media receiving equipment or computers by means of import controls. Third, import substitution policies that affect the pricing structure of hardware can greatly delay the computerization of local firms. Finally, by controlling the telecommunications agency, the government can automatically control the supply of services to the population.

The next chapters provide evidence on the different mechanisms by which the political factor influences diffusion of information technologies.


## NOTES

1. Information technologies are defined as all mechanical or electronic devices—as well as a standard set of procedures—that increase the natural human capability of transmitting, storing, and processing information (Jonscher 1983).

2. Because our main emphasis is the role played by information technologies in state-building processes of developing countries, we are purposely discarding the find-

ings concerning the impact of media on political behavior within the democratic societies of developed countries (Katz and Lazarsfeld 1955; Berelson, Lazarsfeld, and McPhee 1954; Kraus and Davis 1976).

3. "History is both science and philosophy to the extent that we are capable of discovering in it the regularities of human existence" (Preface to the first edition of *Gemeinschaft and Gesellschaft*, in Toennies 1971, 19).

4. Weber considered the only difference between Toennies' distinction and his own to be that "Toennies gave to the terms a more specific definition than I did" (Weber 1971, 41).

5. Aggregate data analysis is defined as a methodology used for studying social phenomena in which "quantifiable attributes of geographical units or transactions among them are compared statistically" (Taylor 1968).

6. This and the following four excerpts are reprinted with permission of the publisher (see Deutsch 1957).

7. This notion is heavily based on Weber's: "La communauté de langue, produit d'une même tradition transmise par la famille et le milieu immédiatement environment, facilite au plus haut point la compréhension réciproque.... Néanmoins, en elle-même, elle ne constitue pas encore une communalisation, mais elle facilite la communication a l'intérieur des groupes en question, et par conséquent elle rend plus aisée la naissance de communalisations.... L'orientation de'après les règles d'une langue commune n'est donc, de façon primaire, qu'un moyen de s'entendre et non un contenu significatif de relations sociales" (Weber 1971, 43).

8. Only a few number of aggregate data analyses of the interaction of communications and development used the number of telephones per 1,000 population as a communications indicator (Alker 1966; Cutright 1963). However, these statistics overlooked the different characteristics of telecommunication networks, as compared to those of mass media.

9. Reprinted with permission of North-Holland Publishing (see Jonscher 1983).

10. This and the following two excerpts are reprinted with permission of the publisher (see Skocpol 1979).

11. The approach we refer to in the study of center and periphery excludes consideration of the functionalist notion that societies have a central structure of values and norms: "Society has a center.... Its centrality, however, has nothing to do with geometry and little with geography. That center, or the central zone, is a phenomenon of the realm of values and beliefs" (Shils 1975, 3).

12. See Katz (1986a).

# 4

# The Impact of Government Policy on the Process of Technological Substitution

The preceding chapter argued that political systems of developing countries shape the national communications environment. This chapter is the first of four dedicated to providing evidence of how politics, rather than economics, determine information technology diffusion. This chapter shows how government policies can shape the national communications system by controlling the process of substitution between competing information technologies.

An information technology does not diffuse in a vacuum, but is introduced within a "communications ecosystem" composed of information technologies that are already supporting societal information flows. When new communication technologies are introduced in a given society, they can support newly created information flows. However, more often, they tend to gain some share of the markets previously supported by older information technologies (Ewing and Salaman 1977). As a result, the level of usage (or "market share") of mature technologies will be determined—at least partially—by the deployment of cost-effective or more attractive substitutes.

The process of substitution of old information technologies by new technologies can be affected by policy mechanisms. As has been thoroughly studied in other cases of technological diffusion, cost-effectiveness and other market-oriented variables influencing adoption can be substantially affected by government policy and regulatory mechanisms.

This chapter explores the role played by government policy in controlling the process of technological substitution between competing communications technologies. Its main argument is that government policy has a direct bearing on the process of technological substitution, by controlling fixed transmission costs (such as mail rates and/or telephone tariffs), or by restricting deployment of new cost-effective technologies.

First, the theory of technological substitution between information technologies is reviewed. Second, the importance of tariffs in explaining traffic substitution of the mail by telephone is explored. Finally, the role of government policy in regulating the process of substitution of the telegraph by the telephone is examined.

## SUBSTITUTION AND COMPLEMENTARITY
## AMONG INFORMATION TECHNOLOGIES

The process of communicating and storing information is considered as being a single, multidimensional one supported simultaneously by several technologies. Information handling tasks (transmission, processing, and storage) are not supported by information technologies on a one-to-one correspondence. Individuals, organizations, and societies transmit, process, and store information by means of multiple technologies deployed within a communications ecosystem. All access factors being equal, a single individual can be linked to his counterparts by mail, telephone, telegraph network, or telex terminal (probably at his workplace)—the "principle of network redundancy". Similarly, he can be reached by means of newspapers, radio, television, or books—the "principle of cumulative impact". Lastly, he might choose to store information in file cabinets, magnetic disks, or tapes—or use a pad, a calculator, or a computer to perform arithmetic calculations—the "principle of functional equivalency".

If the principles of network redundancy, cumulative impact, and functional equivalency are valid, then it is safe to assume that information technologies influence each other in their respective diffusion processes. For example, if a new information technology is deployed and if some of the functions that were being satisfied by a preexistent technology can be fulfilled in a better way or at less cost by the new one, consumers may switch from using the older technology to the new one.[1] This has been called substitution effect, and is usually defined in the communications literature as follows:

Substitution occurs between two communication facilities if a favorable change in the characteristics of one of those facilities exerts, other things being equal, an unfavorable influence on the extent to which the other communication facility is utilized. (UPU 1971, 115)

In economic terms, substitution occurs as a result of a change in the respective shares of the market for communication services. In sociological terms, substitution occurs when an individual decides to adopt an innovation that is perceived as being better than the current technology it supersedes. Although the degree of "relative advantage"[2] of a substitute compared with an older technology is often expressed in terms of economic profitability, it may also be measured in other ways—such as prestige or convenience.

As has been defined above, the concept of substitution assumes two facts:

1. the availability of a "functional alternative" to the information technology being used[3]

2. the cost-effectiveness of that functional alternative

One information technology is a functional alternative to another if two sets of characteristics are common to both technologies: First, from a behavioral perspective, both technologies can help the user to achieve his aims. For example, a user will use video conferencing instead of organizing a face-to-face meeting if the results he expects from the meeting (that is, persuasion of another party) can be achieved by means of the electronic interaction. Similarly, an individual will rely on the television rather than on the newspaper if his objective (such as getting complete information on a certain event) can—ceteris paribus—be similarly achieved by using either medium.

Second, from a physical perspective, both technologies are functional alternatives if technological characteristics and network configurations of the media are similar. For example, in the case of communication technologies, they both have to be available to all parties that need to be reached. Similarly, both technologies have to share the same functionality.

Collins (1980) considers that cost-effectiveness can be determined after total or generalized costs of use are taken into account. According to him, the cost factors that should be assessed for all comparable technologies are fixed costs of terminals and transmission, marginal cost of use, costs of time of operators and users of the technology, and other costs associated with the usage of the technology. For example, in the case of mail, the associated cost is the preparation of the letter; in the case of computing, data entry operations constitute an associated cost. As indicated by Ewing and Salaman (1977), an advantage of the telephone with regard to the mail involves precisely the little cost in preparing for a telephone call as compared to the cost of preparation of a letter, which can often exceed the cost of transmission.

It has also been determined that—while substitution of old technologies by newly diffused ones does generally occur—there are situations in which the newly diffused information technology puts pressure on preexistent ones to adjust and establish a relation of complementarity with the new technology. According to the principle of complementarity, adopters use both technologies equally, to satisfy different but complementary needs. A classic example of adjustment and complementarity is the change introduced in radio broadcasting after the diffusion of television (De Fleur and Ball-Rokeach 1982).

The concept of complementarity was first introduced in the communications literature by Lazarsfeld and Kendall (1960), in their study of the Second National Association of Broadcasters survey of radio listeners. The authors showed that—despite the suggestion that different mass media might compete with each other for their audiences—media tend to complement, rather than compete. Lazarsfeld and Kendall found that audiences for different media tend to overlap:

A radio fan is likely to be a movie fan also, while, conversely, those persons who rarely go to the movies are likely at the same time to be light listeners. (Lazarsfeld and Kendall 1960, 429)

The authors explain this phenomenon by stating that the individual who is interested in a particular content will find that he or she can satisfy that interest better by being exposed to all the media possible, rather than confining attention to one or two of them. Thus, if there is time, such an individual will divide it among the various media.[4]

The notion of complementarity within point-to-point communication technologies was empirically proven in a study prepared for Bell Canada, on the potential of teleconferencing as a substitute for intercity travel (Kollen and Garwood 1975). The study concluded that teleconferencing was more likely to be used as a supplement than as a replacement to travel. According to the study, business travelers did not seem to be interested in substituting teleconferencing for their trips, unless their travel schedule was unusually busy. In that sense, teleconferencing would be complementing face-to-face contact, rather than replacing it.

A special case of extreme complementarity is that of technological parasitism. This is the situation in which the diffusion of a technology is dependent on the deployment of another one. For example, data communications is generally dependent on the development of the telephone network.

There are some patterns of interaction between information technologies that are particular cases of the two effects presented above. For example, the "mushroom effect" (De Fleur 1978) is the phenomenon in which, as a new communication technology is introduced, it is adopted more rapidly than ones that came before. However, this does not mean that the diffusion curve for a new information technology will necessarily be on the next order of steepness. The mushroom effect is a particular case of the substitution effect, in the sense that it is likely to occur when the economic and attitudinal costs for adopting the new technology are lower than those of maintaining the old system.

The "generation effect" is a special case of the phenomenon of complementarity. According to this effect, the increased usage of an information technology may stimulate demand for another technology. For example, the diffusion of the telephone—which can be a substitute for some face-to-face communication—has not caused a decrease in the demand for travel: contrary to this, over the same historic period, the demand for transport has increased manyfold (Short, Williams, and Christie 1976).

In sum, the research literature shows that new information technologies diffuse in an ecosystem where information flows are supported by previously available technologies. Within this process of diffusion, the new technology can substitute the old one, or a relation of complementarity can be created between both. We will now prove that the political variable is key in explaining substitution, and the governments can control the diffusion and substitution process by regulating the cost of utilization of the new technology.

## THE IMPACT OF TARIFFS ON THE
## SUBSTITUTION OF MAIL BY THE TELEPHONE

Ever since the initial deployment of the telephone, the issue of traffic diversion from the mail system to the telecommunications network has been a concern for policymakers, service providers, and communications equipment suppliers.[5] The issue became even more serious when, based on the development of the telephone network, new technologies such as telex and data communications started to diffuse.

The first formal analyses of the impact of the development of telecommunications technologies on postal traffic were carried out in the late 1960s. Sponsored by the Working Party of the Universal Postal Union (UPU)—which was constituted for forecasting demand for postal services in the mid-1980s— several studies were carried out by different PTTs (Postes, Téléphones, et Télégraphes) in the developed world. The studies produced were of different natures—ranging from user survey analysis to the gathering of statistical data and econometric analysis.

For example, the French PTT (UPU 1971) focused its study on the analysis of motivations and behaviors of the two main categories of users of point-to-point communications technologies (business and households), with regard to the various media and their usage habits. The objective of the study was to identify possible competition between the mail and the telephone.

The study concluded that, both in households and in businesses,

the fields of utilization of the letter and the telephone are separate even if they overlap in some cases. Examination of traffic over the last few years reveals a steady growth in both sectors but at different rates. . . . Apart from some special cases in which either the mail or the telephone is used, the combined use of both media predominates. (UPU 1971, 74)

Regarding the specific fields of utilization of each technology, the study concluded that the mail is particularly used in connection with business contracts, private communications based on social conventions, and—in both business and private environments—when the message to be sent is relatively complex or when it contains figures. The study pointed out a relation of complementarity between the technologies. According to the evidence gathered, most telephone messages are confirmed in writing. Conversely, the telephone is used to confirm letter reception.[6]

The Swiss PTTs performed a study based on the analysis of quantitative data. The report examined data on information flows between 1956 and 1966, as presented in Table 4.1. The data show that there is a decrease in growth rate in telegrams sent, and that in 1965–66 domestic mail seemed to grow faster than telephone calls. Based on these data and some international comparisons, the Swiss PTT concluded that telecommunications traffic can be expected to absorb only a small part of the written message volume between 1965 and 1985. The intensity of this limited substitution process in Swiss information

**Table 4.1**
**Growth Rates in Communication Flows in Switzerland**

|  | Average Annual Increase Rate | | |
|---|---|---|---|
|  | 1956-66 | 1960-66 | 1965-66 |
| Local Telephone | 4.9 | 4.7 | 5.0 |
| Trunk Calls | 8.2 | 8.5 | 6.5 |
| Telex Calls (domestic) | 15.7 | 13.4 | 14.7 |
| Domestic Telegrams | 2.7 | 3.1 | 1.2 |
| Letters and Postcards (domestic) | 3.3 | 3.5 | 5.9 |

*Source:* UPU (1971, 81–82).

technologies will be determined by "the degree of saturation and the *possible change in telephone or postal rates*" (emphasis added by author).

Similarly, the Dutch PTTs studied the effect of rates on traffic substitution, by using multivariate regression analysis. They defined the following model:

$$\frac{L_t}{P_t} = e + B_1 \frac{Y_t}{P_t} - B_2 T1_t + B_3 \frac{C_t}{P_t}$$

in which $L_t/P_t$ is number of letters per capita in year t; $Y_t/P_t$ is real national income per capita in year t; $T1_t$ is real letter tariff expressed in cents (index 1960 = 100); and $C_t/P_t$ is telephone calls per capita in year t. The equation yielded the following coefficients and $R^2$:

$$\frac{L_t}{P_t} = 23.5 + 0.3 \frac{Y_t}{P_t} - 0.7 T1_t + 0.05 \frac{C_t}{P_t}$$

$$R^2 = 0.991$$

The result shows that the variable that seems to best explain mail traffic is cost of the technology ($T1_t$). A variable such as usage of the telephone—as measured by the number of calls ($C_t/P_t$)—seems to have very little effect on mail traffic. In addition, the positive value of $B_3$ indicates that—for the Dutch data— the technologies seem to complement each other, and evolve in parallel. A negative $B_3$ would have indicated a phenomenon of traffic diversion from mail to telephone.

In order to search for any substitution effect, the Dutch researchers inverted the equation:

$$\frac{C_t}{P_t} = e + B_1 \frac{Y_t}{P_t} - B_2 T1_t + B_3 \frac{L_t}{P_t}$$

In this case, letter traffic was included as one of the variables explaining telephone traffic. According to the study, a similar phenomenon of complementari-
ness was found. This led the Dutch team to conclude that "competition between
post and telecommunications, in so far as it exists, disappears in face of the
independent growth of letter traffic and telephone traffic" (UPU 1971, 79).
Finally, the study considers that the relation of complementarity between the
mail and the telephone is probably due to the strong relation between mail flow,
telephone traffic, and the social and economic structure.

The general conclusion drawn from these studies was that, in view of the
continual increase in communication flows, substitution by telephone of some
of the postal traffic would be very limited between 1970 and 1985. In addition,
evidence generated by the Dutch and Swiss PTTs proved that substitution
between mail and telephone occurs as a result of rate increases for the usage of
either technology.

In order to replicate the studies of the Dutch and Swiss teams, traffic and rate
data from the United States for the period between 1880 and 1970 was
gathered (all tables are included in Katz 1985). Figure 4.1 presents the number
of messages conveyed by two point-to-point communication technologies in

**Figure 4.1**
**Point-to-Point Communication Flows in the United States, 1880–1970**

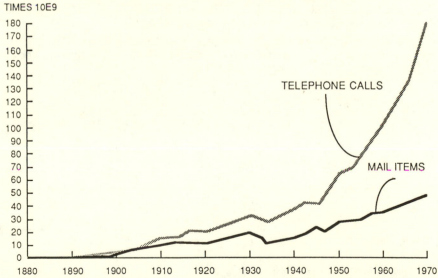

*Note:* Telephone calls include toll and local calls for Bell System and independents. Mail items
         include first class mail and domestic air mail.
*Source: Historical Statistics of the United States.*

the United States between 1886 and 1980 (the telegraph was omitted because of its negligible absolute value).[7] If we assume that a telephone call constitutes a message of the same communication value and meaning as a letter or a telegram (which is certainly debatable), Figure 4.1 shows that—in terms of the number of messages communicated (letters vs. telephone calls)—the telephone exceeded the mail in 1902.

In 1901, approximately half of the annual personal and business messages in the United States were carried by print-based technologies; and the other half, by electronics (telephone and telegraph). Since then, the mail has receded as a point-to-point technology. In 1970, 77.9 percent of the messages in the United States were carried by the telephone; 22.1 percent, by the mail; and 0.03 percent, by the telegraph. These crude statistics exclude the growing electronic-based technologies—such as data communications, facsimile, and telex.

Substitution of mail by telecommunications was also proved in the census of information flows carried out by Pool et al. (1984) on data sets for the United States and Japan between 1960 and 1980. The authors showed that, in both countries, the volume of mail traffic—as measured by words—grew, but at a smaller pace than did electronic point-to-point communications—measured with the same indicator (see Table 4.2). The authors explained that the more rapid growth in electronic point-to-point traffic in Japan is due to the fact that, between 1960 and 1975, the country was achieving full diffusion of the telephone—while the United States had achieved universal penetration of the technology by 1960.

Substitution of mail by telecommunications is driven by costs of respective technologies—which, in the United States, are defined by Congress and the Federal Communications Commission respectively. In order to establish the importance of the cost variable, the model defined by the Dutch research team was run with U.S. data for the period 1886-1970. For that purpose, both

**Table 4.2**
**Growth Rates in Point-to-Point Traffic**

|                           | U.S. 1960-1980 | Japan 1960-1975 |
|---------------------------|:--------------:|:---------------:|
| First Class Mail          | 2.8%           | 4.1%            |
| Electronic Point-To-Point | 6.3%           | 12.8%           |

*Source:* Pool et al. (1984).

variables—cost per piece of mail, and real per-capita income—were considered at 1970 cents and 1958 dollars, respectively. The two models to be tested were the following:

$$\frac{L_t}{P_t} = e + B_1 \frac{Y_t}{P_t} - B_2 T1_t + B_3 \frac{C_t}{P_t} \tag{1}$$

$$\frac{C_t}{P_t} = e + B_1 \frac{Y_t}{P_t} - B_2 T1_t + B_3 \frac{L_t}{P_t} \tag{2}$$

in which $L_t/P_t$ is number of letters per capita in year t; $Y_t/P_t$ is real national income per capita in year t at 1958 dollars; $T1_t$ is real letter tariff expressed in cents (index 1970 = 100); and $C_t/P_t$ is telephone calls per capita in year t. The fit of a curve for data corresponding to the period 1886–1970 in the United States yielded the following result:

$$\frac{L_t}{P_t} = 89.6 + 0.02 \frac{Y_t}{P_t} - 1.9 \, T1_t + 0.30 \frac{C_t}{P_t} \tag{1}$$

$$R^2 = 0.974$$

$$\frac{C_t}{P_t} = 280.93 + 0.05 \frac{Y_t}{P_t} + 5.54 \, T1_t + 2.33 \frac{L_t}{P_t} \tag{2}$$

$$R^2 = 0.987$$

Results for equation (1) show that the variable that seems to best explain mail traffic is cost of the technology. A variable such as usage of the telephone—as measured by number of calls—seems to have very little effect on mail traffic. In addition, the positive value of $B_3$ (0.30) indicates that—for the U.S. data—the technologies seem to complement each other, and evolve in parallel. A negative $B_3$ would have indicated a phenomenon of traffic diversion from mail to telephone. Actually when regressed against mail traffic, a positive coefficient indicates parallel growth:

$$\frac{C_t}{P_t} = 3.79 \frac{L_t}{P_t} - 200.9$$

$$R^2 = .9103$$

The interest in equation (2) resides in the value of $B_2$ (5.54). This shows that replacement of first-class mail by the telephone is enhanced by the increase in postal rates, relative to telephone rates (Ewing and Salaman 1977). In fact—while demand for first-class mail is quite inelastic—repeated rate increases render demand more elastic, and cross-elasticities between demand for mail and telephone develop:

$$\frac{C_t}{P_t} = -194.70 + 0.18 \ \frac{Y_t}{P_t} - 6.98 \ TC_t + 3.62 \ Tl_t$$

$$R^2 = .9578$$

in which $TC_t$ is real telephone tariff. Increases in mail rates directly affect telephone traffic. Similarly, telephone rate reductions directly influence traffic:

$$\frac{C_t}{P_t} = -210.74 + 1.37 \ \frac{L_t}{P_t} + 0.18 \ \frac{Y_t}{P_t} - 0.76 \ TC_t$$

$$R^2 = .9524$$

As the coefficients of the equations show, government policy has a direct bearing on the process of technological substitution, by controlling fixed transmission costs (such as mail and telephone tariffs). The variable that seems to best explain mail traffic is real letter tariffs, which is directly controlled by the government. A consequence of an increase in the letter rate is that some messages are no longer sent by post, but transmitted by telephone. Conversely, an increase in the telephone rate leads to replacement of telephone calls by letters. In summary, the importance of government intervention in the shaping of this process of technological substitution—by means of rate fixation—has been underscored.

## GOVERNMENT POLICIES AFFECTING SUBSTITUTION AMONG COMPETING COMMUNICATIONS TECHNOLOGIES

We have analyzed the role of governments in regulating diffusion of information technologies by controlling their cost structure. In other instances, governments can prevent diffusion of information technologies not, indirectly, by regulating the cost structure but, directly, by introducing legal restrictions.

One of the most extreme examples is provided by the French government—which resisted the introduction of the electric telegraph, in order to protect the optical telegraph. In France, the development of the electrical telegraph proceeded slowly, because the government was reluctant to abandon its system of optical telegraph. By 1842, when Morse applied for a license to build a commercial system, the government operated more than 3,000 miles of optical telegraphs. Once the electrical telegraph was introduced in 1852, its development was controlled by military and other government needs, and not by commercial demand.

In a similar reaction, most of the European governments adopted a highly conservative attitude toward the diffusion of telephone technology, in order to protect their investment in the telegraph. For almost all European governments, the telegraph was a known technology with substantial plant investment. The telephone was a new technology with unknown demand and uncertain operating characteristics. As Brock argues,

Rapid development of long-distance telephone would have caused telegraph capital losses if it had been very successful and potential telephone capital losses if it had been unsuccessful. Either result could cause political problems for the government agency. (Brock 1981, 146)

To counter the potential competitive threat, the emerging telephone systems were placed under the control of the telegraph agency—giving birth to the PTTs. Thus, by exercising the public policy imperative, the European governments controlled the impact of a new technology on both the market and the industry organization.

For example, in 1887 when the French government completed a Paris-Brussels telephone link, the resulting drop in telegraph traffic aroused the government's concern. In order to protect its telegraph revenues, the French government delayed further long-distance construction. As a result, French long-distance telephone was unreliable and limited in coverage, for more than a quarter of a century.

In England—as in France—the government impeded telephone development. However, the mechanisms for government control of the diffusion of telephone technology were different from those in France. Up to 1880, the government prohibited private development. Between 1880 and 1891, telephone systems were allowed to be installed privately, under a regime of short-term licenses. After 1891, the government started developing its own system, but charged tariffs substantially higher than those of the telegraph. These three policies extended the life of the telegraph technology, relative to long-distance telephone technology. As a result, the British long-distance network remained very underdeveloped at the time of nationalization in 1911.

In Germany, the government—rather than seeing the telephone as a competitor to the telegraph—viewed it as a complementary device that would serve to extend telegraph service to places that were too small to support a telegraph office.

Because the telephone did not require a skilled operator, a public telephone could be placed in a village with a line to the nearest telegraph office so that telegraph messages could be called in. (Brock 1981, 140)

Exchanges were installed by the government in 1880, in order to preempt the market from earlier attempts by Bell to establish a private company. Consistent with the "complementarity" approach, long-distance telephone lines were built only where demand exceeded the capacity of existing telegraph facilities.

The national expansion of the German telephone system was prevented because the telegraph administration was afraid that lower telephone rates would decrease its revenues (Brock 1981). When new rates were established in Germany in 1900, a rapid expansion of the telephone service started especially in the smaller cities.

In summary: for a certain period, European governments acted as a conservative force restricting the diffusion of a new information technology that represented a potential threat to existing state-operated media. The introduction of a competing, superior, and cheaper technology—such as the telephone—generally results in the decline of existing technologies—such as the telegraph. This is what happened in the United States where conditions of competition existed, and less dramatically in European countries where the telegraph was a protected monopoly.

Are governments of developing countries playing the same role that the Europeans did during the last century? In the developing world, the decline of the telegraph has been a much slower process, due to government intervention. When the government also controls the telephone agency—which is the case in most developing countries—the state assumes a typically risk-averting behavior with regard to the introduction of the new technology. If the government were to rapidly develop a long-distance telephone network, this would cause capital losses to the telegraph system. As a consequence, the general response adopted by most governments is to initiate slow development of a long-distance network—which constitutes both a response to potential criticisms of government inaction, and a way of protecting telegraph investment. As Brock asserts,

A technological innovation [is] not allowed to break down established market power, capital values, rate structures, or operating procedures developed in the telegraph. The changes [come] in slow, measured steps rather than the abrupt shocks to the status quo that are induced by market forces during technological revolutions. (Brock 1981, 147)

The underdevelopment of the telephone network leads to increased usage of the telegraph in order to channel a portion of the total information flow, which tends to grow as a result of economic growth.

The same phenomenon can be identified in the relationship between the mail and the telephone. If the process of substitution of print-based technologies by electronic-based technologies as described for the industrialized world is universal, a statistical analysis performed on a worldwide representative range should show a negative correlation between the diffusion of the telephone and mail traffic. In addition, all electronic-based technologies should repeat the same relationship with mail traffic, which is a typical print-based technology.

Table 4.3 presents correlation coefficients among all point-to-point technologies for a sample that varies between 79 and 120 nations of the world.

With the exception of the telegraph, the diffusion of telecommunications technologies seems to be correlated with mail traffic. Table 4.3 shows that, for 1980, countries that have high mail traffic tend to score high telephone and telex density. The explanatory power of this statement is very limited. The high correlation among all these indicators may be due to the fact that economic development is correlated with usage of information technologies. Structural factors—essentially economic and demographic—always determine an in-

**Table 4.3**
**Correlation Coefficients among Point-to-Point Technologies**

|  | TELEPHONE DENSITY | TELEGRAPH USAGE | MAIL USAGE | TELEX SUBSCRIBERS |
|---|---|---|---|---|
| TELEPHONE DENSITY | --------- | 0.068 (100) | 0.881 (94) | 0.684 (120) |
| TELEGRAPH USAGE | | | 0.079 (79) | 0.000 (97) |
| MAIL USAGE | | | ---------- | 0.560 (88) |
| TELEX SUBSCRIBERS | | | | ---------- |

*Note:* The sample size is indicated between parentheses.
*Source:* Data from ITU (1982); United Nations (1982); and UNESCO (1982). Analysis by the author.

crease in the need to communicate. This was precisely one of the explanations provided in the UPU studies reviewed above. Thus, a developing country will always score high in the usage of all information technologies—both print based and electronic.

The reasons why there is no significant decline in mail flows—and thus no negative correlation between print-based and electronic-based information technologies—are three: First, the decrease in utilization of print-based technologies can only be measured as a function of total information flows, when determined by a standardized indicator, such as the number of words (Pool et al. 1984).[8]

Second, it can be assumed that the reason there is no negative correlation—but positive—does not constitute a methodological problem, but is an expression of reality. In short, it can be hypothesized that at a worldwide level an increase in diffusion of electronic-based technologies does not lead—at least in principle— to a decrease in usage of the mail. For example, in a typical developing country, the leapfrogging phenomenon leads to diffusion of the telephone long before usage of the mail as a communication technology has achieved a saturation point. In that sense, two S-curves would be overlapping: Figure 4.2 shows that, during period e, diffusion of the telephone does not significantly influence usage of the mail. The aggregate information flow is growing; and, thus, the telephone is not gaining market share at the expense of the mail, which still has a possibility of growth because the aggregate information flow is growing.

**Figure 4.2**
**Parallel Diffusion Processes of Information Technologies**

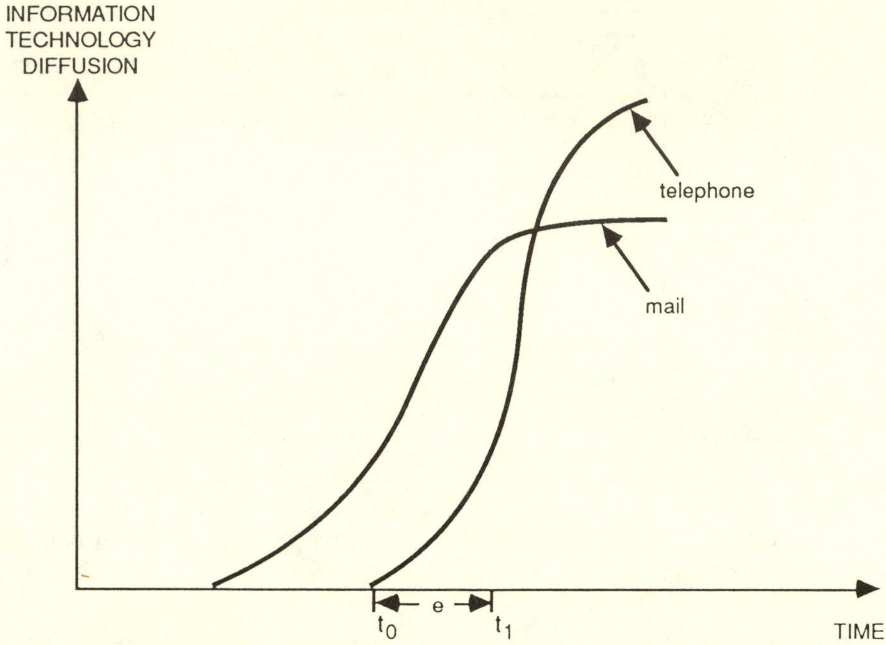

INFORMATION
TECHNOLOGY
  DIFFUSION

telephone

mail

$\leftarrow e \rightarrow$
$t_0$          $t_1$                                              TIME

*Source:* Author.

It can also be assumed that the principle of generation is present. Accordingly, while the diffusion of the telephone is diverting part of the print-based flow, it is also generating flow and, therefore, compensating for the substitution. Finally, even though there are cross-elasticities, it is difficult to measure the extent of the substitutability, because the two services are not identical in the functions they provide.

We have shown how governments, both in developed and developing countries have had a significant influence in either delaying or fostering diffusion of an information technology such as the telephone.

## CONCLUSION

Point-to-point information flows tend to increase in most countries—either determined by economic growth, or independently from fluctuations in the economy. Within this context, a process of traffic diversion is in place, by which electronic technologies tend to channel a growing share of the information flow. This process of traffic diversion from print-based to electronic point-to-point communication technologies is shaped by political factors, in most countries of the world.

In many cases (such as the telegraph), it is the state that will temporarily restrict the diffusion of new, more efficient technologies to protect established rights in already available transmission methods. In other cases, the state will control the process of substitution by either price mechanisms or service supply regulation. In summary, a complex pattern of reinforcement and substitution among information technologies is being shaped not only by economic and attitudinal factors, but also by political and regulatory variables.

## NOTES

1. For further analysis, see Porter (1980, 23–24).
2. See Rogers and Shoemaker (1971).
3. De Fleur and Ball-Rokeach (1982) developed the term "functional alternative" to explain the decline of the cinema when television started to diffuse.
4. In the literature on the use of mass media for socioeconomic development, the effect of complementarity has been called "centripetal":

Media participation, in every country we have studied, exhibits a centripetal tendency. Those who read newspapers also tend to be the heaviest consumers of movies, broadcasting, and all other media products. (Lerner 1963, 341)

5. While this section focuses on traffic diversion from print-based to electronic communications systems, it is worth mentioning that substitution and competition within print-based, point-to-point technologies can also occur. For example, this was the case in the emergence of a private courier industry in the United States in the mid-1830s—which led, in turn, to the tightening of government postal monopoly (Ewing and Salaman 1977).
6. These remarks should be reexamined today in light of the diffusion of the facsimile.
7. Similar charts have been generated by Pool et al. (1984) for shorter series.
8. If we take a look at "hard" indicators of information flows—such as number of letters—we see that the number of domestic mail items handled annually in the United States is actually increasing. It is only when Pool et al. (1984) normalize the indicators by number of words and compare with the aggregate information flow that the declining trend in print-based media traffic appears. Thus, the only way to analyze the presumed universality of the technological substitution between mail and telecommunications would be to standardize traffic indicators—such as telephone calls or mail-items handled—to a common measurement—such as words. The problem that this type of analysis would convey is that of a cultural idiosyncratic nature—the hidden assumption being that a letter or a telephone call contains the same amount of words throughout the world. This hampers the inference of meaning from any cross-sectional time series or—even worse—a cross-sample.

# 5

# The Impact of Government Policy on Information Technology Transfer

Chapter 4 presented evidence on the role governments play in shaping national communications and information environments, citing the specific case of government policy driving processes of communications traffic diversion from print-based to electronic point-to-point technologies. This chapter discusses another way political systems influence information technology diffusion: the transfer of technology across national borders.

We argue that the international diffusion of information technologies is determined in large part by existing patterns of power, influence, and resource allocation policies in each of the adopting nations, as well as the relation of both economic and political interdependencies. The chapter explains the mechanisms by which politics can influence information technology transfer. As an example, a case study is presented showing how the Brazilian government affected the domestic rate of computer diffusion by enacting an import substitution policy.

## POLITICS AND INTERNATIONAL DIFFUSION OF INFORMATION TECHNOLOGIES

It has been argued—particularly by trade theorists—that, in the process of international diffusion of technology, two steps are involved: intercountry transfer, and intracountry diffusion of the technology. Intercountry transfer is the process by which a technology is introduced into a country. Intracountry diffusion focuses on the diffusion process within each of the adopting countries (Tilton 1971).

In addition to this two-step process, diffusion of technologies occurs at two levels: among users, and among producers. International diffusion among users

Table 5.1
Characteristics of International Diffusion of Information Technologies

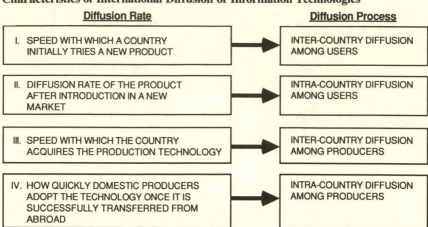

Diffusion Rate                                    Diffusion Process

I.  SPEED WITH WHICH A COUNTRY          →    INTER-COUNTRY DIFFUSION
    INITIALLY TRIES A NEW PRODUCT            AMONG USERS

II. DIFFUSION RATE OF THE PRODUCT       →    INTRA-COUNTRY DIFFUSION
    AFTER INTRODUCTION IN A NEW              AMONG USERS
    MARKET

III. SPEED WITH WHICH THE COUNTRY       →    INTER-COUNTRY DIFFUSION
    ACQUIRES THE PRODUCTION TECHNOLOGY       AMONG PRODUCERS

IV. HOW QUICKLY DOMESTIC PRODUCERS      →    INTRA-COUNTRY DIFFUSION
    ADOPT THE TECHNOLOGY ONCE IT IS          AMONG PRODUCERS
    SUCCESSFULLY TRANSFERRED FROM
    ABROAD

*Source:* Author, based on Tilton (1971).

starts when consumption in countries other than the innovating one is satisfied by foreign imports. Diffusion among producers occurs when firms within countries other than the innovating one start to manufacture the product.

The concepts of intercountry transfer of technology, intracountry diffusion, and diffusion among users are usually utilized for assessing a country's performance in the transfer of any technology. In order to do so, four aspects are analyzed, as presented in Table 5.1.

The diffusion of a typical information technology generally starts in developed countries. This is due to two factors: First, the scientific and technical resources needed to develop new products and industrial processes are heavily concentrated in those technically advanced countries. Second, the existence of a potential demand arising from a higher standard of living and larger market size provides the producers in developed countries with a unique advantage in developing new products (Linder 1961; Pavitt and Wald 1971; Johnson 1968). In addition, market demand may also come from government activities, such as military and space programs.

After successful introduction in the innovating country, the export trade of the innovating firms fosters significant demand for the product in foreign countries that have similar structures of demand. At this point, the innovating country generally has a monopoly in the international trade of the product. Since the product enjoys high income elasticity of demand, exporting originally takes place to other countries with high income and a similar pattern or demand structure (Wells 1972).

As the product matures, foreign production—either by a local firm or by direct foreign investment of the innovating firm—begins. This generally occurs first in other developed countries. Their technical capabilities and resources permit the early identification of significant foreign developments and facilitate the transfer of technology. In addition,

because the structure of demand is similar in advanced countries, there is a strong incentive for adopting innovations introduced in other advanced countries. (Tilton 1971, 20)

These two conditions for early adoption of technology at the international level have also been identified at a microlevel, in the research on the individual characters of adopters in the diffusion of innovations. In their review of the diffusion literature, Rogers and Shoemaker (1971) showed that early adopters are—among other characteristics—wealthier, more specialized, and belong to larger size units (that is: bigger firms, larger farms, and so on). The authors explain that

Some new ideas are costly to adopt and require large initial outlays of capital. Only the wealthy units in a social system may be able to adopt these innovations.... Because the innovator is the first to adopt, he must take risks that can be avoided by later adopters. Certain of the innovator's new ideas are likely to fail. He must be wealthy enough to absorb the loss from these occasional failures. (Rogers and Shoemaker 1971, 87)

According to trade theory, the lag occurring between the moment a product is introduced in the innovating country and the moment it is adopted in another country (the "demand lag") is determined by the size of the economy of the adopting country. In general, the larger the size of the economy of the adopting country, and the greater the similarity in the structure of demand between the imitating and the innovating country, the shorter the demand lag will be.

Two other variables will influence the length of the demand lag: the usefulness and price of the innovation as compared to the one being substituted, and the height of trade barriers. These factors will also condition the process of intracountry diffusion among users. Consistent with this definition of demand lag, the literature on diffusion of innovations has established that the rate of adoption is a linear function of the profitability of employing the innovation, the size of the investment required to use it, as well as other unspecified variables (Mansfield 1968).

Intercountry diffusion among producers—like intercountry diffusion among users—depends on the type of technology, as well as characteristics of the adopting countries. For example, the less technically sophisticated the new product is, the less the need for follow-up on research and development. Also, the smaller the economies of scale and the shorter the producer learning curve, the faster domestic production will start (Freeman 1973; Hufbauer 1966).

Similarly, the time-span for starting domestic production (the "imitation lag") will tend to be shorter, the greater the potential comparative advantage of the adopting country, the lower the barriers to its exports, the larger its domestic demand for the product, and the harder it is for imports to meet this demand.

It may also happen that developing countries attract the eventual transfer of the new technology by their lower wage rates—thus reducing the imitation lag. However, this process is usually slower than the transfer to advanced countries. In general, transfer to developing countries will only occur after the product has matured, and the most intensive factor input has changed from skilled labor to capital (Majumdar 1982). Lastly, among determining factors of the rate of diffusion on the producer side is the accessibility of licensing and technical assistance agreements with foreign producers.

Interestingly enough, the importance of political factors as a variable conditioning international diffusion of technologies is very seldom mentioned in the trade theory literature. These few instances have been mainly made in connection with the analysis of industrial policy formulations and their impact on trade policy. Anderson and Baldwin (1981), for example, mention some of the "noneconomic" reasons for the formulation of an industrial policy: (1) a collective desire for industrialization, (2) national security, or (3) the fostering of a "particular" way of life.

In general terms, politics can influence international diffusion processes at all steps. However, diffusion among producers, the step that leads to local production of the technology, is probably the most sensitive to state intervention. National security appears to be one of the key factors in accelerating, by means of political intervention, the international diffusion among producers. Given the importance held by information technologies in the national security of a given country, it is expected that state intervention will occur almost inevitably, at certain stages of development, to foster local production of those technologies.

When it comes to diffusion among users, government policy is usually one of many possible factors. While government policy can regulate utilization of information technologies, their adoption is mainly driven by the country's structure of demand (see Chapter 6). However, there are cases when government policy aimed at stimulating local production ("diffusion among producers") has significant impact on diffusion among users. For example, import substitution policies may affect equipment pricing and, as a result, delay diffusion among users.

In the next section, we will analyze the formulation of the market reserve policy for minicomputers in Brazil, which occurred in the late 1970s. Initially driven by national security considerations, the policy was aimed at stimulating local production of minicomputers. As the analysis shows, the policy had an initial negative impact on the diffusion rate of computers in the Brazilian economy.

## THE CASE OF COMPUTERS:
## POLITICS AND DIFFUSION IN BRAZIL

The rate of diffusion of computers is highly sensitive to the purchase price and operating cost of the capital goods in which they are embodied (Mansfield 1968).[1] As Rada states,

The high cost of equipment clearly hinders diffusion of computers. Inasmuch as they are not used by small enterprises and services, they are less competitive with manual methods and amortization takes longer. (Rada 1981, 22)

Similarly, Stoneman—in his 1976 study of the diffusion of computer usage in the United Kingdom—determined that the extent of adoption of computing is related to the economy's output and computer prices. Chow (1967) had also indicated the same, when studying the spread of computing in the United States.

Diffusion of computers at a worldwide level is highly correlated with the macroeconomic indicator of GNP. When GNP per capita is correlated against computer density for 73 countries of the world, the correlation coefficient is 0.57 (see Figure 5.1). As the figure indicates, the richer a nation is, the higher the computer density will be.

However, economic factors only partially explain diffusion levels of computing. Certain government policies may act as an obstacle for diffusion of computers. For example, if computer diffusion is related to equipment pricing, an import substitution policy that leads to an increase in price or a radical shift in

**Figure 5.1**
**Computer Density vs. per Capita GNP for 45 Countries, 1980**

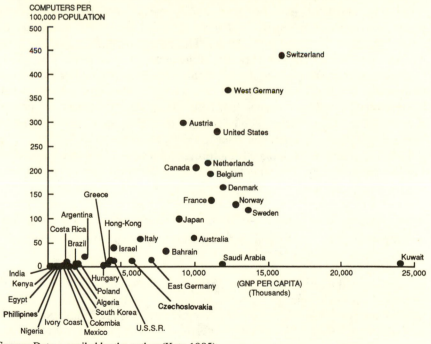

*Source:* Data compiled by the author (Katz 1985).

product mix will necessarily hinder adoption of computers by local firms. Such was the case in Brazil between 1977 and 1979.

In the early 1970s, Brazil ranked first among the Latin American countries in the number of computer installations. With 754 systems installed by 1971, it claimed 26.49 percent of the total installations on the continent (Barquin 1974). The computer systems—all imported—came from a variety of sources, with IBM clearly the dominant supplier. At this time, the foreign dominated computer industry with absolutely no domestic participation, and the implications for national security gained increasing attention.

The first steps in the development of a national computer policy came in 1970, when the Brazilian Navy—stronghold of nationalistic sentiments—decided to modernize its fleet and to buy six new frigates with digital, computerized systems. The navy sought a vendor that would not only provide the systems, but also create a maintenance service in Brazil and build a computer manufacturing plant.

In conjunction with its search for a foreign supplier of computer technology, the navy created by decree a Special Task Group (*Grupo de Trabalho Especial* or GTE) in February 1971. The group—jointly organized and coordinated by the minister of the navy and the minister of planning—would encourage the development and building of a prototype of electronic computer for naval operations.

In parallel to GTE's efforts to create a national computer industry, the Brazilian government created an agency to control the acquisition of computers by the federal government. By 1972, federal agencies owned 20 percent of the approximately 800 computers in Brazil. These state-owned computers varied considerably in their origins, brands, languages, and standards. The newly created agency would pull together and rationalize government computer activities. In 1972, the *Commissao de Cordenacao des Atividades de Processamento Electronico* (CAPRE) was created to organize censuses of computer equipment, give advice on the purchase of computers by federal agencies, and coordinate all training activities in computer science existent in Brazil.

In the meantime, GTE looked for a foreign joint venture partner for producing computers locally. The conditions of the agreement sought by GTE were the following:

- no restrictions on the export of equipment build in Brazil by the joint venture;
- free transfer of updated technology and eventual ownership of the transferred technology to *Equipamentos Electronicos* (a Brazilian company).

GTE contacted eight foreign firms. AEG/Telefunken and Phillips were not interested—given the terms of the agreement. Hewlett-Packard would not accept being only a minority interest in the venture. Digital Equipment Corporation contested the conditions for transferring technology. From the remaining four firms (Varian, Ferranti, CII, and FUJITSU), GTE chose two: Ferranti—the candidate supported by the navy, since it provided the computers for Brazilian ships; and FUJITSU—which was supported by the minister of planning and the National Development Bank.

At that point, conceptions within GTE of the way in which Brazil's national computer industry should develop began to diverge. The National Development Bank and the Ministry of Planning agreed that the Brazilian industry should satisfy the demands of the market—both military and civilian—while the navy thought the military market should be given priority. The navy finally conceded; and GTE decided on the creation of a pilot company, comprised of *Equipamentos Electronicos*, the National Development Bank, and two foreign partners. It would manufacture products for both the military and civilian markets.

When the Geisel administration came to power in 1974, the institutional basis of Brazil's national computer policy consisted of two state-owned companies and a supervisory agency. DIGIBRAS was a national holding company responsible for the development of computer peripheral devices. COBRA was a state-owned computer manufacturer engaged only in research and development. CAPRE continued as the agency responsible for analysis of the planned expansion of the government data-processing center.

Thus, between 1971 and 1974, the process of defining a Brazilian computer policy was mainly conducted by two partners: a political entity—the Brazilian state; and, at the policy's origins, a military entity, the Brazilian Navy. The private sector was virtually absent from the initial efforts to promote development of a domestic computer industry.

The active role of the state and the absence of the private sector represent two aspects of the same problem. First, on the one hand, the Brazilian private sector has characteristically tended to invest in areas of low risk and short-term return on investment—leaving the state to invest in those areas that required large amounts of capital and provided only gradual return on investment over the long-term.

Second, on the other hand, the increasing investment of the public sector in the economy was mainly directed at the development of considered strategic industries for national development—such as oil, nuclear energy, and aeronautics. In addition, the state also subsidized national manufacturers in an attempt to reduce the price of domestically produced goods and induce their participation. Thus, the lack of investment by the private sector in research and development of new technologies was the consequence of the paternalistic tradition of the Brazilian state. A "spontaneous" development of science and technology—based on investments in the private sector—never materialized in Brazil. Applied research has resulted only from the state intervention.

The state's willingness to promote a national computer industry derived from political determination, rather than economic need. This was first broadly outlined by Brazilian President Costa e Silva at an Organization of American States (OAS) conference in Punta del Este (Uruguay) in 1967. President Costa e

Silva defined the development of science and technology as a principal means for attaining economic development in Third World countries—emphasizing the need for Latin American countries to increase their effort in nuclear research, despite opposition from the developed nations. Costa e Silva perceived technological development not as a substitute for foreign sources of technology, but as a way of enhancing the developing nation's bargaining power with developed countries in the acquisition of high technology products.

During 1976, CAPRE's political power over the computer industry continued to grow. A decree issued in February 1976 by the minister of planning restructured CAPRE and gave it explicit responsibility for defining a national computer policy. According to this decree, a collective body would direct CAPRE. A plenary council was given the responsibility of designing the general lines of a national computer policy. CAPRE's plenary council immediately established that the domestic industry could not compete with the prices or the technology of the large foreign vendors, and that Brazil as a country could do without their "superfluous" or state-of-the-art technology. Hence, CAPRE decided to create national Brazilian oligopolies with fully protected positions in specified conventional Brazilian markets. The minicomputer and small business systems groups were reserved exclusively for domestic firms with international companies denied access.

The plenary council specified in detail the workings of the market reserve policy for minicomputers. A limited number of companies would be approved. Initially, local firms were allowed to buy the technology of the foreign companies with such purchased technology limited to a 4–5 year life span. Subsequent models had to be developed locally. The minicomputer firms could not diversify the production of computer products, but had to concentrate on the central processing unit (CPU)—leaving other companies the opportunity to manufacture peripherals and all other computer products. Standard interfaces were a strict requirement. The plan allowed the possibility of opening the minicomputer market to foreign competition at a later time.

In December 1977, the Brazilian government selected three domestic firms to manufacture minicomputers and sell them in the Brazilian market. At the same time, hoping to reverse the government's decision to prohibit foreign participation, seven multinational corporations submitted proposals—all rejected by CAPRE.

The market reserve policy had a decisive impact on the rate of diffusion of computing among Brazilian firms. Table 5.2 shows the evolution of computer distribution by size, between 1972 and 1980. The number of computers installed in Brazil increased from 1,779 in 1972 to 8,444 in 1980. The market for all computers grew at a rate of about 35 percent a year in 1975 and 1976. The rate dropped to 16.2 percent in 1977 and 11.4 percent in 1978, partly as a result of CAPRE's controls on imports of medium and mini-computers. Therefore, these restrictions, which were imposed even before a full range of nationally produced models was available in Brazil, had reduced the supply of computers.

**Table 5.2**
**Computer Distribution by Size, Brazil, 1972–80**

| | VERY LARGE | | LARGE | | MEDIUM | | SMALL | | SUBTOTAL | | MINI | | TOTAL | GROWTH OVER LAST FIGURE CONSIDERED |
|---|---|---|---|---|---|---|---|---|---|---|---|---|---|---|
| | N | % | N | % | N | % | N | % | N | % | N | % | N | |
| December 1972 | 25 | 1.4 | 23 | 2.1 | 185 | 10.3 | 467 | 26.2 | 700 | 39.3 | 1,079 | 60.6 | 1,779 | |
| July 1973 | NA | NA | NA | NA | NA | NA | NA | NA | NA | NA | NA | NA | 2,391 | 34.5% |
| July 1974 | 42 | 1.5 | 71 | 2.5 | 289 | 10.4 | 781 | 28.3 | 1,183 | 42.9 | 1,573 | 57.0 | 2,756 | 47.0% |
| July 1975 | 61 | 1.6 | 82 | 2.1 | 332 | 8.8 | 1,052 | 27.8 | 1,527 | 40.3 | 2,266 | 59.7 | 3,793 | 37.6% |
| July 1976 | 72 | 1.4 | 99 | 4.9 | 338 | 6.6 | 1,309 | 25.5 | 1,818 | 35.4 | 3,313 | 64.6 | 5,131 | 35.3% |
| December 1976 | 82 | 1.4 | 109 | 1.9 | 349 | 6.2 | 1,270 | 22.9 | 1,816 | 32.7 | 3,734 | 67.2 | 5,550 | 8.1% ⎤ 16.2% |
| July 1977 | 87 | 1.5 | 122 | 2.1 | 353 | 5.9 | 1,296 | 21.7 | 1,858 | 31.2 | 4,105 | 68.8 | 5,963 | 7.4% ⎦ |
| December 1977 | 92 | 1.4 | 134 | 2.1 | 356 | 5.6 | 1,333 | 20.9 | 1,915 | 30.1 | 4,434 | 69.8 | 6,349 | 6.4% ⎤ 11.4% |
| July 1978 | 93 | 1.4 | 166 | 2.5 | 370 | 5.6 | 1,378 | 20.7 | 2,007 | 30.2 | 4,634 | 69.8 | 6,641 | 4.5% ⎦ |
| December 1978 | NA | NA | NA | NA | NA | NA | 1,392 | 19.5 | NA | NA | 5,111 | 71.7 | 7,123 | 7.2% ⎤ 12.7% |
| July 1979 | 97 | 1.2 | 226 | 3.0 | 377 | 5.0 | 1,494 | 19.9 | 2,174 | 29.0 | 5,294 | 70.6 | 7,488 | 5.1% ⎦ |
| July 1980 | 23 | 1.8 | 248 | 2.8 | 388 | 4.8 | 1,600 | 19.0 | 2,359 | 26.6 | 6,397 | 72.3 | 8,844 | 18.1% |

*Source:* Compiled by the author from: CAPRE, *Buletim Tecnico* 1(January/March 1979):71; CAPRE, *Buletim Informativo* 1(April/March 1973):45; CAPRE, *Bulletim Informaivo* 3(July/August 1975):6; DATA NEWS 115(March 1981):22; and *Gazeta Mercantil,* October 24, 1979.

**Table 5.3**
**Growth Rate of the Brazilian Minicomputer Market**

| 1974 | 67.0% |
|------|-------|
| 1975 | 44.0% |
| 1976 | 46.2% |
| 1977 | 23.9% |
| 1978 | 12.8% |
| 1979 | 14.2% |
| 1980 | 20.8% |

*Source:* Katz (1981).

Yet, despite this relative stagnation in the overall market, the market for large computers grew by an impressive 36 percent in 1978. However, this rate represents an increase of only 44 units, with an average price of US$900,000 per unit. The customers were companies with relatively large data processing operations.

More important in the analysis of the market trends is the growth rate of the minicomputer market; and here the impact of Brazil's market reserve policy is indisputable (see Table 5.3). The growth rate fell abruptly in 1977 and 1978. Growth increased in 1980, but still reached less than half the 1976 level.

However, during this time period there was a rising demand for mini-computers, due to two main reasons. First, growth of firm size brought about the need for greater information handling, and created a variety of new applications. Because the import of large equipment was tightly controlled, users alleviated some of their labor-intensive business processes—such as payroll, billing, and inventory control—by using minicomputers. Second, new users were brought into the market by an increasing competitive environment, which required greater productivity utilizing the information-handling capabilities of the minicomputer if firms were to remain competitive.

This increasing demand for minicomputers was constrained, as evidenced by the annual growth rates of CPUs (by size) between 1976 and 1980 (see Table 5.4). Government import restrictions on medium and small-sized computers and particularly, the market reserve policy for minicomputers, shifted demand away from the potentially large market for minicomputers as well as small and

**Table 5.4**
**Market Growth Rate by Size of Computers, Brazil**

|      | VERY LARGE | LARGE | MEDIUM | SMALL | MINI | TOTAL |
|------|------------|-------|--------|-------|------|-------|
| 1976 | 18.0       | 20.7  | 1.8    | 24.4  | 46.2 | 35.3  |
| 1977 | 20.8       | 23.2  | 4.4    | (1.0) | 23.9 | 16.2  |
| 1978 | 6.8        | 36.0  | 4.8    | 6.3   | 12.8 | 11.4  |
| 1979 | 4.3        | 36.1  | 1.8    | 8.4   | 14.2 | 12.7  |
| 1980 | 26.8       | 9.7   | 2.9    | 7.0   | 20.8 | 18.1  |

*Source:* Compiled from government statistics. See Katz (1981).

medium-sized computers and toward the market for large systems. CAPRE also affected the growth rates of markets for larger systems in other ways. During 1978 and 1979, CAPRE systematically advised users who sought import approval for very large systems to instead consider buying large systems. In short, Brazilian computer policy during the late 1970s shifted demand to the large systems by damping demand in size ranges above and below that market.

This government-induced shift in demand worked to the detriment of the overall market. Since minicomputers were not available in the market, many small and medium-sized businesses continued to rely on manual processing. Their operating budgets did not allow the option of investing in more automated systems. Thus CAPRE's policy diminished the size of the market.

Observers estimated the Brazilian market for computers and peripheral equipment at US$112.4 million in 1975 (see Table 5.5). Imports accounted for more than 95 percent of this market ($107.3 million). Moreover, 90.9 percent of production—which reached $55.8 million in 1975—came from IBM's "drawback" operations in its Brazilian manufacturing plant, where the firm produced its "370" line almost exclusively for export. Thus, "real production"—that destined for the internal market—accounted for little more than $5 million—less than 5 percent of the potential market. The remainder of domestic computer production in 1975 went to export markets.

Two years later—in 1977—the size of the Brazilian market for computers and related equipment changed considerably. It is evident from Table 5.5 that the market size dropped to less than half of the 1975 level. Production levels in 1977 reflected a net decrease of 6.6 percent from the levels of 1975. Mean-

**Table 5.5**
**Size of Brazilian Market for Computers and Related Equipment**
**(in thousands of U.S. dollars)**

|  | 1975 | 1976 | 1977 |
|---|---|---|---|
| PRODUCTION | 55,800 | 39,070 | 52,160 |
| IMPORTS | 107,340 | 34,050 | 45,300 |
| EXPORTS | 50,740 | 33,930 | 41,800 |
| MARKET SIZE | 112,400 | 39,190 | 55,660 |

*Source:* Katz (1981).

**Figure 5.2**
**Comparison of Brazilian Domestic Computer Production and**
**Number of Installations Sold per Year**

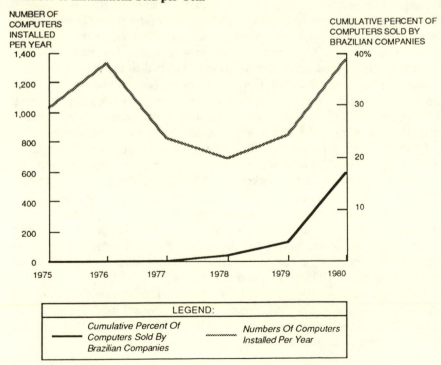

*Source:* Katz (1981).

while, import levels dramatically decreased, at a rate of 57.8 percent. Therefore, the decrease in imports accounted for 51.2 percent of the reduction in
the market size. This contraction was due to blanket import restrictions
imposed earlier by CACEX (the Brazilian Foreign Trade Department)—
which were subsequently adapted to the peculiarities of the computer market
by CAPRE in late 1975. That year, CAPRE not only controlled computer
imports on a case-by-case basis, but also instituted a ceiling on overall computer imports. In 1976, this ceiling was placed at $80 million; and in 1977, at
$100 million.[2]

Since 1977, imports have increased; and, since 1979, CAPRE and SEI
(Secretaria Especial de Informatica) have progressively raised the ceiling on
imports. In 1978, it was raised to $138 million; and in 1981, to $280 million—
which included a $1 million ceiling on components for assembly in Brazil.
These increases did not mean a liberation of import control, but rather should be
considered with inflation rates in mind.

Figure 5.2 summarizes the impact of the market reserve policy on the diffusion of computers in its first years of application. It compares the total number
of computers installed per year whether produced by foreign or domestic companies with the sales of domestic Brazilian companies between 1975 and 1980.
As can be seen, during 1978 and most of 1979, domestic production was
limited, because most Brazilian companies had not yet reached massive production levels. This had an important effect on the market: Imports were regulated
and, therefore, the foreign offering was reduced. The market decline in 1978
and 1979 results from the depressed offering of domestic companies, which
were not prepared to satisfy the requirements of the market. Not until the end of
1979 did Brazilian firms begin to produce minicomputers.

Thus, a portion of the Brazilian economy had to continue using manual
information systems. Small businesses, which the policy affected most severely,
were not able to buy minicomputers until the end of 1979. And when they
became available, the hardware was sold at a higher price than equivalent
equipment on the international market. Furthermore, the newly created industries did not have the capability to satisfy the market's needs. Thus, demand
remained constrained for a certain period of time.[3]

## CONCLUSION

The Brazilian case presents an example of government policy affecting the
diffusion rate of an information technology by modifying variables such as
market access and pricing structure. As stated at the beginning of this chapter,
the process of international diffusion is composed of four steps: intercountry
diffusion among users, intracountry diffusion among users, intercountry diffusion among producers, and intracountry diffusion among producers. As we
stated in the case of Brazil, politics, although seldom mentioned in the research
literature, may exert a decisive impact on each of the steps composing the
process of international diffusion.

In Brazil, we have encountered a typical case of political factors influencing the diffusion of computers. By 1977, the country had successfully introduced the technology ("intercountry diffusion among users"). However, the political decision to initiate local production ("intercountry diffusion among producers") had an initially negative impact on the rate of diffusions of the technology among the users ("intercountry diffusion among users"). The issue arises whether the increase of local supply during the 1980s has corrected for the initial deficiencies. Some analysts argue that, although local supply had grown, pricing of medium-sized computers in Brazil remains higher, in relative terms, than what can be found in the international market. Therefore, the import substitution policy may still be exerting a negative impact on the process of diffusion among users of computing.

In sum, this chapter has analyzed how governments influence the international diffusion of an information technology among private users. In the next chapter, we expand our evidence on the significant role of politics in information technology diffusion with an example of how governments themselves adopt information technologies, and influence the process of diffusion.

## NOTES

1. Analysis of the worldwide diffusion of computing has to be based on a differentiation between at least two distinct products, which—while sharing technical characteristics and functions—are designed to be diffused within different populations of adopters. On the one hand, there are the general purpose computers and minicomputers. These devices are typically purchased by organizations of various sizes and generally provide data processing services to a multiplicity of users. On the other hand, the professional and home computers—although they may be purchased by either organizations (corporations or universities) or individuals—are specifically designed to provide computing services to the individual.

One should bear in mind that there is no clear-cut separation between the two types of products, in terms of market segments. Yet, the assumption of a differentiation needs to be made, when measuring levels of diffusion—so as not to equate a microcomputer in a developing country to a large mainframe in an industrialized nation.

2. The difference in 1977 between imports of $45.3 million and the ceiling of $100 million reflects the fact that the data in Table 5.5 does not include parts and components imported for maintenance and assembling purposes. These were included in the import ceiling and were estimated at about $42 million for 1977.

3. The market reserve policy had a much larger impact than only restricting the rate of diffusion of computers. Issues such as job creation, backward linkages, and relative technological autarchy should also be included in a larger assessment of the Brazilian computer policy and its implications for the domestic economy.

# 6

# "Non-Economic" Variables as Drivers of Diffusion of Information Technologies among Governments

Chapter 6 discusses a special case of intercountry diffusion of information technologies. It focuses on the adoption of technologies by governments. The term "adoption" describes in this case either the usage of a technology by the government, the implementation of a technology by a public agency, or the enactment of legislation requiring the public sector to operate a new technology. Thus, adoption is defined as the decision leading to the introduction of a new technology in a given country.

First, we discuss the theoretical and methodological implications of diffusion among governments, as opposed to individuals. Second, we present evidence of the key role played by the political system, using the case study of the international diffusion of television broadcasting. Finally, a specific example is presented: the adoption of television broadcasting by African governments.

## THEORETICAL AND METHODOLOGICAL ISSUES IN THE STUDY OF DIFFUSION PROCESSES AMONG GOVERNMENTS

Research on diffusion of innovations—defined as the process by which new products, processes, or ideas spread to the members of a social system—started in the mid-1950s (Griliches 1957). Since then, most of the research has been performed by sociologists and economists (Rogers and Shoemaker 1971) who were focusing on the diffusion of physical objects, programs, or organizational innovations. Research has particularly emphasized the personal traits of potential adopters or the collective sociological traits of multiperson adopters (such as large organizations), the social relationships among innovators and imitators, and the relative importance of different channels of communication. In addition, sociologists have studied significant characteristics of innovations, as they are perceived by potential adopters.

The study of diffusion processes among governments started to develop in the late 1930s. Yet, the contributions remain rather scarce when compared to other areas of diffusion research. In 1940, McVoy published an article on the diffusion of the city-manager form of government with cities of the United States. The study was based on the hypothesis that diffusion of innovations followed a geographical pattern, by which diffusion processes result from spatial proximity.

The impact of geographical propinquity on policy diffusion processes has been widely studied. Sharkansky—in his 1970 study of regionalism in the United States—identifies three factors that explain and support the diffusion of public policies among neighbor governments. These are: (1) similarities in conditions and problems, (2) the belief that it is legitimate "to adapt one's own programs to those of nearby governments," and (3) frequent interaction among officials of neighboring polities. When studying policy diffusion in the international arena, spatial or geographic diffusion was redefined to mean not only territorial propinquity, but also political affiliation. For example, when studying worldwide diffusion of social security policies, Collier and Messick (1975) determined that international organizations and agreements may play an important role in the policy diffusion process. Similarly, Leichter (1983) showed that political communities—such as the British Commonwealth— provide a framework within which the diffusion of policies has more geographical latitude. This is particularly important because

"Nations" cannot always look to their neighbors for guidance on appropriate policy models. Neighbors do not always share similar problems or material conditions. And even when they do, it may be that one's neighbor provides neither a model nor guidance in the policy area. (Leichter 1983, 226)

The imitation of policies based on common cultural and socioeconomic factors—rather than geographic proximity—has been called "lateral diffusion" (Leichter 1983, 232).

In summary, the two single factors that influence the policy diffusion process within the international arena are spatial proximity and the sharing of communication networks within a community of extranational affiliations. The combination of these two factors had already been studied by Crain (1966) in his doctoral dissertation on the diffusion of fluoridation among cities. Working under the influence of the "two-step flow" hypothesis (Berelson, Lazarsfeld, and McPhee 1954; Coleman et al. 1957; Katz and Lazarsfeld 1955), Crain determined that a pure geographic pattern of diffusion is not valid in the presence of modern communications. He argued that the diffusion of an innovation among governments requires not only information formally communicated, but information and social support delivered through informal channels—such as social interaction between policymakers.

Crain drew an analogy between the decision maker within the government and the physician studied by Coleman et al. (1957):

The physician realizes that there is always risk in the use of a new drug. He also recognizes the vested interest of both the drug salesman and the research worker in his acceptance, and hence is reluctant to adopt on their recommendations alone. However, he has neither the time nor the skill necessary to evaluate the drug personally. [Thus], the doctors discuss the problem, and reduce the ambiguity of the situation by making what amounts to, in Lewin's terms, a "group decision." (Crain 1966, 469)

Based on this assumption, Crain showed that, in the case of fluoridation, peer-group influence—in the form of policymakers of cities having adopted the innovation—played an important role in its diffusion. Thus, according to Crain, the process of policy diffusion was less dependent on spatial considerations, but was heavily based on personal contact among policymakers. The concept of spatial proximity was translated into a principle explaining policy diffusion. This principle was called "copy your neighbor" (Leichter 1983; Collier and Messick 1975).

The "copy your neighbor" principle can be found in different situations. For example, a neighbor government adopts an innovation because it shares similar problems or material conditions as the previous adopter—it acts with an imitation purpose. Or because, in copying the neighbor, the adopting country is retaliating—within an antagonistic and competitive context.

A second model of policy diffusion is that of hierarchical diffusion (Collier and Messick 1975). In the case of hierarchical diffusion, innovations appear in the most advanced or largest centers, and are then adopted by successively less advanced or smaller units. This process has been observed in the diffusion of semiconductor technology among nations (Tilton 1971), fluoridation techniques among U.S. cities (Crain 1966), and policies among U.S. states (Walker 1969; Gray 1973). A special case of hierarchical diffusion is initiated and encouraged by the more developed nations—as Leichter (1983) showed for the diffusion of land registration laws among British Commonwealth nations.

In addition to these specific characteristics, intercountry diffusion research is in need of differentiating itself from diffusion processes occurring at the micro level, in terms of the assumptions that underly any typical diffusion model. For example, one of the cornerstones of conventional diffusion research is the S-shaped curve, which defines the nature of the learning and imitation dynamics that constitute the diffusion process.

As Warner explains,

Assuming that adequate supplies of an innovation are available, and that knowledge of the innovation's existence is widespread, the specification of the [S-curve] implies that potential users initially approach the adoption decision with caution: that they experiment with the innovation on a trial basis... and wait for feed-back—from their own experimentation and from the reports of other users—on the innovation's costs, value, and so on, before deciding whether or not to adopt. Later, as more and more positive feedback accrues, both lack of knowledge of how to best use the innovation and uncertainty about the results of using it are reduced, and the pace of the adoption process increases. (Warner 1974, 436)

It is clear from Warner's description that the central assumption that underlies the S-shaped diffusion model is the social interaction among adopters and nonadopters over time. In that sense, the S-curve is no more than a Gaussian distribution-based model arising from the absence of any dominant factors, under the law of large numbers.

While it can be safely assumed that some of the learning and imitation processes described above may occur in intercountry diffusion (that is, government officials interacting with their counterparts and transmitting information about an innovation), the S-curve model cannot be applied for studying diffusion among countries. First, it is impossible to use the S-curve for analyzing diffusion among a limited number of adopters, such as approximately 150 countries. Second, the underlying assumption that, under an S-shaped process, no single variable other than social interaction can explain the phenomenon is not valid for intercountry diffusion. As Downs and Mohr argue,

Diffusion curves may strongly suggest that communications-related variables are important for innovation, but they do not demonstrate the importance, nor do they quantify it, especially in relation to causes of other types. We emphasize this because we have observed a recent tendency, especially among political scientists, to assume that because the diffusion of a particular innovation takes the shape of an S-curve when graphed, a knowledge of the communication network within the adopting population will explain the variations in innovativeness. (Downs and Mohr 1976, 711)

This is precisely the point that Perry and Kraemer (1979) criticize in Gray's 1973 study of the diffusion of public policies among the U.S. states. Gray explains policy diffusion mainly by assuming that "leaders from each adopter state come in contact with leaders from each non-adopting state" (1973, 1176) in a random fashion, and that there is no constant source from which the innovation is diffused. However, if the random social interaction assumption is rejected and, on the contrary, we assume that there is a single diffusion source (the federal government, in Gray's case), the S-shaped curve cannot provide a test of theoretical validity.

Under such an assumption—that, instead of random social interaction among government officials, there is a constant source from which the innovation is diffused to the adopting population—an epidemiological model of diffusion would be more appropriate. According to this model,

the diffusion process forms an essentially geographical pattern and can be visualized as a succession of spreading ink-blots on a map created by the initial adoptions of new policies by states playing in a national "league" of cue taking and information exchange, followed by other states whose standards of comparison and measures of aspiration are more parochial and who typically adopt new policies only after others within their "league" have done so. (Walker 1969, 1187)

Diffusion processes among countries or governments have specific character-istics that differentiate them from more conventional processes of diffusion. While some factors can be utilized in explaining diffusion in both cases, con-cepts such as spatial proximity or retaliatory imitation are mainly applicable to the explanation of diffusion among governments. The fact that the processes of diffusion of innovations are social phenomena that involve economic, sociolog-ical, and political factors is currently admitted (Warner 1974; Mansfield 1968; Perry and Kraemer 1979). Yet, in the case of intercountry diffusion of informa-tion technologies, variables like "profitability" and "channels of communica-tion between adopters" would seem to be less important than political variables.

As it might be expected, the particular importance of political factors affects the methodological constructs that are utilized for analyzing intercountry diffu-sion of information technologies. By using only the population of a country as potential adopters of information technologies, and explanatory variables such as literacy, urbanization, and average income (see Chapter 3), we might obtain an incomplete explanation of the diffusion process. Such a model omits one of the most powerful determining variables: the political.

In fact, a study that deals with information technologies diffusion should necessarily consider government policy as a key factor in both the intercountry and intracountry diffusion processes. By focusing on the political aspect of government adoption of information technologies, we are establishing a theoretical difference from most studies that explain national communications and information systems growth. These studies—which have been considered part of the "prerequisites explanation" approach (Collier and Messick 1975)—generally focus on the level of social and economic modernization as an expla-nation for the diffusion of information technologies within countries (Cutright 1963; Alker 1966; Lerner 1958; McCronne and Cnudde 1967).

The differences between a prerequisite approach and a policy diffusion explanation are twofold: First, while acknowledging that certain prerequisites emerging from the economic and social systems are generally a condition for communication systems growth, the policy diffusion approach considers that an understanding of the diffusion process might shed some light on why some nations adopt information technologies earlier than others. In that sense, a "particular threshold level of modernization is a necessary, but not a necessary *and* sufficient condition for adoption" (Collier and Messick 1975, 1304, emphasis added by author). The policy diffusion approach complements the prerequisites framework by studying the factors that influence the adoption of a given policy in a given country but also extend beyond the frontiers of a national community. This approach will be utilized for studying specific ex-amples of the international diffusion of television.

## POLITICS AND GOVERNMENT ADOPTION
## OF TECHNOLOGY: THE EXAMPLE OF
## TELEVISION BROADCASTING

The information technologies most commonly in the decision domain of governments are those of mass communications. In addition to the specific characteristics of intercountry diffusion processes described above, the diffusion of mass communication technologies is differentiated by specific traits not shared by other innovations. First, the diffusion of point-to-mass information technologies is the result of two parallel diffusion processes: among transmitters and among receivers. Second, at least one of these two processes is highly influenced by the political variable—national communications policy or industrial policy.

A mass communication system, which is supported by different information technologies, is a complex structure that includes a source of messages and several receivers. As a result, the growth of a communication system in terms of its audience or nodes is directly determined by the type, strength, and quality of the message sent. Therefore, the diffusion of mass communication technology is—in general—a process determined by the adoption of transmitting technology by the source, and the adoption of receiving devices by the receivers. In economic terms, one could argue that the diffusion of an information technology occurs at the supply and demand level. This is precisely what Lerner meant, when he argued that

to evaluate the functioning of a communication subsystem within a societal system, it is essential to consider—it may even be wise to begin with—the conditions that determine the efficient functioning of all economic processes; the capacity to produce and the capacity to consume. (Lerner 1963, 336)

Lerner defined the capacity to produce as the investments in plant, equipment, and personnel that allow the production and distribution of information via mass media. The author stated that

No country—whether its ideology be Hamiltonian, Stalinist, or Gandhism—can produce information via mass media until it has an economic capacity to construct and maintain the physical plant of the mass media. (pp. 336–37)

Conversely, the capacity of a population to consume mass media products was linked by Lerner to three variables: income level, literacy, and "motivation."

These two parallel diffusion processes—at the source level and at the receiver level—are particularly relevant when analyzing cross-national diffusion processes. In the case of certain information technologies, diffusion of supply technologies should be differentiated from diffusion of technologies conceived for receiving messages. For example, if we consider the diffusion of broadcasting, we can assume that intercountry diffusion among users may first occur via import of shortwave radios to receive broadcasts from overseas. Then, the introduction of transmitting technologies would represent further inter-country diffusion among users. Once this happens, radios could be increasingly imported to satisfy domestic market needs (intracountry diffusion of receiving technologies among users). At a certain point, the government may decide that a local industry of radio receivers should be developed. This would mean intercountry diffusion of receiving technologies among producers. Finally, the cycle would be closed when domestic manufacturing of transmitters starts (intercountry diffusion of receiving technologies among producers).

The concept of double diffusion processes has been empirically analyzed by Frey (1973). In his study of communications development, he described what happens when major industrialized nations decide to adopt an innovation:

In the course of about five years such nations can move from virtually no television to one set for every ten persons, and in another ten years can essentially provide a set for every family. (Frey 1973, 351)

Frey implicitly alluded to two parallel processes of diffusion of innovations: one, among countries; and the second, within the population of every country. Both processes closely interact. Thus, a country's communication policy can shape the pattern of growth of a given medium. For example, the way the television audience in a given country grows will directly depend on the decision the government makes concerning the moment to initiate television broadcasting and the rate of increase of its transmission capacity. Thus, the transmitting power constitutes a supply constraint in the diffusion of television receivers.

### Worldwide diffusion of television

Frey (1973) considered television diffusion to have all the characteristics of an innovation in the early stages of its diffusion process. Worldwide aggregate

**Table 6.1**
**Worldwide Diffusion of Television Broadcasting**

NUMBER OF COUNTRIES WITH THE FOLLOWING NUMBER OF
TELEVISION SETS PER 1,000 POPULATION

|      | Number Of Countries With TV | 0.1– 1.99 | 1.99– 10.99 | 11– 20.99 | 21– 50.99 | 51– 100.99 | 101– 199.99 | 200– And + | Data Not Found |
|------|------|------|------|------|------|------|------|------|------|
| 1960 | 82  | 19 | 20 | 6  | 10 | 7  | 4  | 4  | 12 |
| 1970 | 123 | 20 | 13 | 13 | 14 | 15 | 17 | 23 | 8  |
| 1980 | 138 | 14 | 21 | 10 | 9  | 18 | 27 | 39 | 0  |

*Source:* Compiled by the author, based on UNESCO data (1982).

figures provide evidence for this assertion. The process of diffusion—as depicted in Table 6.1—has the particularity of being composed by two parallel subprocesses: one, among countries; and the second, within the population of each country. While television technology has diffused rapidly among countries, diffusion within each country has proceeded at a slower pace. For example, in 1960, 18 percent of the countries running television services had more than 50 sets per 1,000 population. In 1970, the percentage of countries with more than 50 sets per 1,000 had risen to 45 percent. Finally, in 1980, the percentage of countries with an equivalent penetration level was 61 percent.

In reality—as indicated above—both processes of diffusion closely interact. For example, the way the television audience in a given country grows will directly depend on the moment in which the government decides to initiate regular television broadcasting and on the rhythm of increase of the system's transmission capacity. We will first focus on the diffusion among countries (or intercountry diffusion), and second on the diffusion within their respective populations (or intracountry diffusion).

The international diffusion of television technology has occurred in the past 30 years. Despite the fact that some countries started broadcasting regular programs in the mid-1930s, television is essentially a postwar phenomenon. In 1950, only 5 countries had a regular television broadcasting system. In 1955, there were 17; and in 1970, the number had climbed to 123. In 1979, the number of countries and dependent territories having regular television broadcasts was 138 (UNESCO 1982).

**Figure 6.1**
**Worldwide Diffusion of Television**

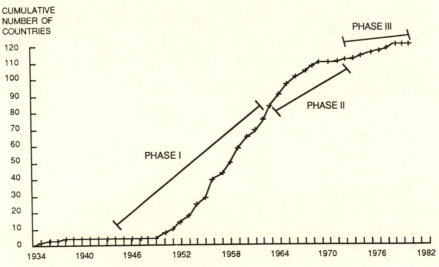

*Source:* UNESCO (1982). Analysis by the author.

In order to trace the diffusion process among countries, a curve that plots the adoption dates known for 120 countries and territories[1] was drawn as Figure 6.1. The figure shows that the international diffusion of television started after World War II. The process can be divided into three stages: Between 1946 and 1962, almost all industrialized countries and advanced developing countries adopted the technology. The second stage—which developed between 1962 and 1970—was determined by the adoption of television by those newly created nations that had enough resources to afford regular broadcasts. Finally, the third stage started in the 1970s, with the adoption by small and lesser developed countries.

Some aspects of these three stages are shown in Figure 6.2, in which the percentage of adopting countries and territories is plotted by continent. Using a sample of 136 adopting countries and territories, the percentage of adopters was calculated for each year according to the total number of countries and territories by continent.[2] Europe achieved almost complete diffusion by 1964.

**Figure 6.2**
**Percentage of Countries with TV System, 136 Countries by Continent, 1934–80**

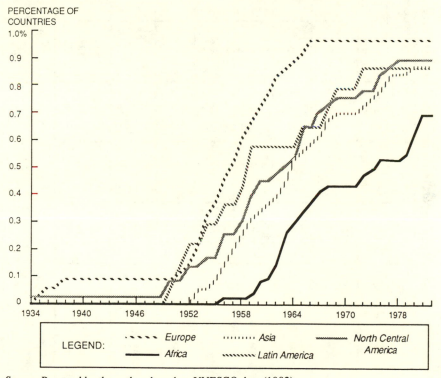

*Source:* Prepared by the author, based on UNESCO data (1982).

Table 6.2
Distribution of Countries According to the Number of Television Receivers per 1,000 Inhabitants, by Continent, 1960–79

| Continent | Year | Total Number Of Countries | Number Of Countries With The Following Number Of Receivers Per 1,000 Inhabitants | | | | | | |
|---|---|---|---|---|---|---|---|---|---|
| | | | At Least One | 2 to 10 | 11 to 20 | 21 to 50 | 51 to 100 | 101 to 200 | More Than 200 |
| AFRICA | 1960 | 5 | 3 | 2 | — | — | — | — | — |
| | 1976 | 31 | 11 | 9 | 3 | 6 | 2 | — | — |
| | 1979 | 36(9)* | 1 | 9 | 4 | 5 | 3 | 1 | — |
| NORTH AMERICA | 1960 | 14 | 2 | 6 | 3 | — | 1 | — | 2 |
| | 1976 | 27 | — | 3 | 2 | 4 | 6 | 4 | 8 |
| | 1979 | 29 | — | 1 | 1 | — | 6 | 8 | 10 |
| SOUTH AMERICA | 1960 | 8 | 2 | 2 | 2 | 2 | — | — | — |
| | 1976 | 12 | — | 1 | 1 | 2 | 5 | 3 | — |
| | 1979 | 12 | — | — | 2 | 2 | 1 | 7 | — |
| ASIA | 1960 | 17 | 7 | 9 | — | — | 1 | — | — |
| | 1976 | 30 | 2 | 5 | 4 | 6 | 4 | 7 | 2 |
| | 1979 | 30(3)* | 1 | 3 | 2 | 4 | 4 | 5 | 5 |
| EUROPE | 1960 | 24 | — | 5 | 3 | 8 | 5 | 2 | 1 |
| | 1976 | 32 | — | 1 | — | — | 1 | 9 | 21 |
| | 1979 | 33 | 1 | — | — | 1 | — | 6 | 24 |
| OCEANIA | 1960 | 2 | 1 | — | — | — | — | 1 | — |
| | 1976 | 6 | — | — | — | — | 1 | 2 | 3 |
| | 1979 | 8 | — | — | 1 | 1 | — | 3 | 3 |
| WORLD TOTALS | 1960 | 70 | 15 | 24 | 8 | 10 | 7 | 3 | 3 |
| | 1976 | 138 | 13 | 19 | 10 | 18 | 19 | 25 | 34 |
| | 1979 | 148 | 3 | 13 | 10 | 13 | 14 | 30 | 42 |

*The number in brackets is the number of countries that had less than one receiver per 1,000 inhabitants.

Note: In 1979, for 4 countries in Africa, from a total of 40; for 3 countries in North America, from a total of 32; for 3 countries in Asia, from a total of 33; for 1 country in Europe, from a total of 34, the information on number of receivers was not available.

Source: UNESCO (1982, 23).

In 1980, the only European territory that did not have TV was the Vatican. South America was the second continent to have adopted television in almost all its countries and territories. The only two exceptions being the Falkland (*Malvinas*) Islands and Guyana. In North and Central America, adoption stabilized by 1975, with 29 out of the 36 countries and territories having regular television services. Africa is a clear example of the two later stages in the international diffusion trend. The first period extends between 1960 and 1968, while the second one started in 1971 and is still ongoing. Asia shows a different pattern: continuous diffusion until 1975, when 83 percent of the countries were running television services. Therefore, with the exception of Africa,

**Table 6.3**
**Diffusion of Television in Selected Developed Countries**
**(Measured in Number of Sets per 1,000 Population)**

| YEAR | UNITED STATES | JAPAN | EAST GERMANY | WEST GERMANY | FRANCE | UNITED KINGDOM |
|---|---|---|---|---|---|---|
| 1955 | 227.0 | ... | 0.8 | 5.0 | 6.0 | 105.0 |
| 1956 | ... | ... | ... | ... | ... | ... |
| 1957 | ... | ... | ... | ... | ... | ... |
| 1958 | ... | ... | ... | ... | ... | ... |
| 1959 | ... | ... | ... | ... | ... | ... |
| 1960 | 307.7 | 72.9 | 60.0 | 83.6 | 41.6 | 211.5 |
| 1961 | 310.3 | 97.4 | 85.2 | 104.8 | 55.4 | 220.1 |
| 1962 | 316.3 | 131.6 | 110.6 | 126.7 | 72.9 | 228.8 |
| 1963 | 326.8 | 156.5 | 138.7 | 142.3 | 92.0 | 237.8 |
| 1964 | 349.7 | 170.9 | 164.9 | 172.0 | 112.1 | 242.9 |
| 1965 | 326.1 | 182.9 | 189.0 | 192.8 | 133.1 | 247.9 |
| 1966 | 377.0 | 190.4 | 208.6 | 213.8 | 152.0 | 254.1 |
| 1967 | 392.5 | 198.5 | 230.2 | 230.5 | 167.8 | 271.1 |
| 1968 | 396.1 | 206.2 | 244.3 | 248.5 | 185.4 | 279.8 |
| 1969 | 399.7 | 213.9 | 249.6 | 264.2 | 201.8 | 285.5 |
| 1970 | 412.9 | 219.3 | 263.8 | 275.9 | 216.0 | 294.1 |
| 1971 | 449.2 | 244.0* | 272.5 | 280.0 | 227.4 | 297.4 |
| 1972 | 474.0 | 271.0* | 282.8 | 295.3 | 237.5 | 304.2 |
| 1973 | 556.1 | 297.6* | 292.5 | 300.9 | 236.6 | 308.7 |
| 1974 | 571.0 | 330.7* | 296.9 | 307.4 | 235.2 | 320.0 |
| 1975 | 586.0 | 358.3* | 310.0 | 311.7 | 268.3 | 330.0 |
| 1976 | ... | ... | 311.0 | ... | 271.7 | 361.0 |
| 1977 | ... | ... | ... | ... | ... | ... |
| 1978 | ... | ... | ... | ... | ... | ... |
| 1979 | 635.0 | 469.0 | 336.0 | 335.0 | 341.0 | 399.0 |
| 1980 | 626.9 | 539.3 | 342.4 | 337.9 | 354.6 | 404.0 |

*Note:* Data for Table 6.3 has been obtained from UNESCO sources and represent either estimates or number of licenses issued per year. In that sense, all cross-country comparisons should be very cautious. The analysis focuses more on diffusion patterns than on *the density of sets per country.*
*Source:* UNESCO (1982).

television broadcasting has achieved almost total penetration among countries and territories of the world.

While adoption by countries seems to be a universal phenomenon, diffusion among their respective populations shows several imbalances related to country specificities (see Table 6.2). Regarding the diffusion process of receivers among the world's population, Frey (1973) drew two conclusions. First, along with Canada, the United Kingdom, and—more recently—Sweden, Germany, and Japan, the U.S. distribution of television receivers has seemingly stabilized, and will remain at roughly the same level until new patterns of usage develop or a new competitive medium arises. Second, there are signs of what one might call a premature stabilization of distribution in television receivers at what seem essentially elite levels in many developing countries.

In light of data for the past decade in the developed countries, our analysis supports Frey's first conclusion, showing that with the exception of the United States, Japan, and the United Kingdom—the other developed countries seem to have reached a saturation point at around 300 sets per 1,000 population. Only in the United States has television density increased beyond the "300 point," which was reached in the early 1960s (see Table 6.3). However, as to Frey's second assertion about a premature stabilization in the process of diffusion of receivers within developing countries, evidence is mixed. Some countries have—as Frey argued—a premature saturation point, while others are still adopting television sets.

**Figure 6.3**
**Diffusion of Television in the United States, 1946–80**

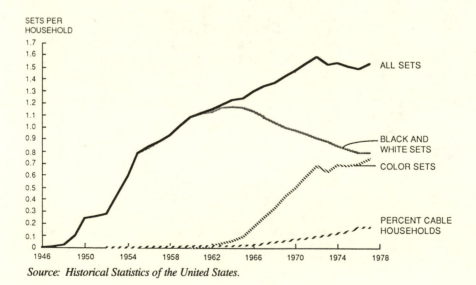

*Source: Historical Statistics of the United States.*

As Frey (1973) predicted, a new pattern of usage in the United States—as well as new technological developments—have kept television diffusing beyond an initial saturation point. Figure 6.3 shows that, by 1960, there was an average of one television set per household. The first development that pushed for increased adoption of receivers was color television. By 1965, the purchase rate of monochrome sets started to decline, due to reductions in the cost of color sets. In addition, the development of cable TV, low-power TV, and video cassettes determined further increases in the television density. This would also apply for Japan and the United Kingdom.

In the other industrialized countries included in Table 6.3, the slow or nil development of cable TV by 1980 had an impact on the diffusion process. Future analyses of penetration time series will certainly show the impact of recent develop-

**Table 6.4**
**Diffusion of Television in Selected Developing Countries**
**(Measured in Number of Sets per 1,000 Population)**

| YEAR | NIGERIA | BRAZIL | MEXICO | SOUTH KOREA | ALGERIA |
|------|---------|--------|--------|-------------|---------|
| 1955 | 0.00 | 1.20 | 3.80 | 0.00 | 0.00 |
| 1956 | . . . | 2.30 | 5.50 | . . . | . . . |
| 1957 | . . . | 3.40 | 9.20 | . . . | . . . |
| 1958 | . . . | 5.20 | . . . | . . . | . . . |
| 1959 | . . . | 6.40 | 17.20 | . . . | . . . |
| 1960 | 0.02 | 8.50 | 18.60 | 0.30 | 5.60 |
| 1961 | 0.14 | 10.50 | 24.90 | 0.80 | 6.10 |
| 1962 | 0.22 | 14.20 | 24.90 | 1.20 | 6.20 |
| 1963 | 0.22 | 17.50 | 27.00 | 1.20 | 6.10 |
| 1964 | 0.30 | 21.20 | 28.20 | 1.20 | 6.00 |
| 1965 | 0.60 | 24.70 | 29.50 | 1.60 | 6.70 |
| 1966 | 0.80 | 28.10 | 35.50 | 1.70 | 7.70 |
| 1967 | 0.80 | 31.90 | 40.50 | 2.80 | 7.40 |
| 1968 | 0.90 | 37.40 | 47.00 | 5.20 | 7.20 |
| 1969 | 1.00 | 43.70 | 54.20 | 8.20 | 7.70 |
| 1970 | 1.30 | 49.60 | 62.00 | 13.00 | 10.80 |
| 1971 | 1.30 | 56.10 | 64.50 | 21.60 | 13.70 |
| 1972 | 1.30 | 63.90 | 70.40 | 29.90 | 16.50 |
| 1973 | 1.40 | 74.10 | 77.20 | 39.30 | 25.20 |
| 1974 | 1.50 | 85.00 | 84.00 | 48.60 | 29.80 |
| 1975 | 1.60 | 95.30 | . . . | 57.70 | 30.30 |
| 1976 | 1.60 | 106.50 | . . . | 66.40 | . . . |
| 1977 | . . . | 117.70 | . . . | . . . | . . . |
| 1978 | . . . | 128.60 | . . . | . . . | . . . |
| 1979 | 5.70 | 141.20 | 111.60 | 151.00 | 47.00 |
| 1980 | 5.80 | 152.70 | . . . | 167.70 | 52.40 |

*Source:* UNESCO (1979; 1982).

ments of cable television in West Germany and France. This would lead us to conclude that changes in the regulatory environment (such as the development of cable television) have an important effect on the pattern of diffusion of television.

Turning now to the developing countries, Table 6.4 includes time series on television sets per 1,000 population for five developing countries, chosen as representatives of different levels of development. Table 6.4 shows the difference in diffusion patterns between Brazil, Mexico, and South Korea on one side; and Algeria and Nigeria, on the other. In 1960, Brazil and Algeria had a relatively similar level of penetration of television sets; two decades later, penetration in the former was three times higher than in the latter. The difference is even more surprising when we compare the evolution of income levels per capita for both countries, and find almost equivalent income levels from 1957 to 1981, as shown in Table 6.5.

This rough comparison indicates that the diffusion of television sets is a function of factors other than average income level. Other variables that can explain television diffusion, include program characteristics, signal strength, purchase credit requirements, and relative cost of the equipment (Bain 1962)—as well as regulatory variables, such as equipment import restrictions and industrial policy related considerations, such as local manufacturing capacity.

Overall, however, the income level would seem to be a dominant factor explaining variance in penetration levels of TV sets. In regressing GNP per

**Table 6.5**
**Income Level Comparison between Brazil and Algeria**

|        | GNP per capita in U.S. Dollars | |
|        | BRAZIL | ALGERIA |
|--------|--------|---------|
| **1957** | 293 | 178 |
| **----** | | |
| **1980** | 2,160 | 1,940 |
| **1981** | 2,220 | 2,140 |

*Source:* World Bank (1982); Russett et al. (1964).

**Figure 6.4**
**Television Density vs. per Capita GNP, 47 Countries, 1980**

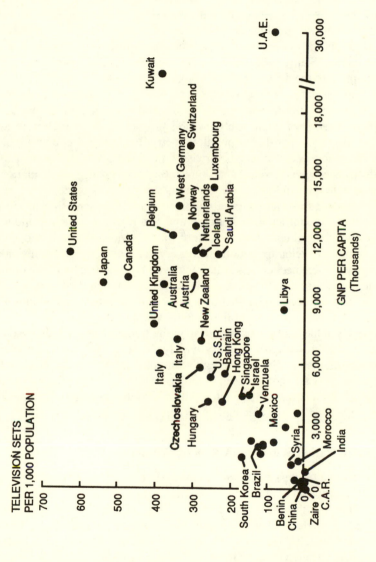

*Source:* Prepared by the author, based on World Bank (1982); UNESCO (1979; 1982) data.

capita against penetration of TV sets for 47 countries we find a relatively clear correlation. While the squared correlation coefficient between both variables is only 0.358, its low value is due primarily to the presence of such "outliers" as the oil-producing countries—with high GNP and low television receiver density (see Figure 6.4).

However, the scattergram also shows a number of countries that are clearly below the penetration level, given their income levels. In addition to the economic variable, technological innovation or changes in the characteristics of service might have a potential impact on the diffusion of sets—as was shown for the United States. In Brazil, for example, the introduction of color TV gave new impulse to the diffusion of television.

Therefore, with the exception of Africa, television broadcasting has achieved almost total penetration among countries and territories of the world. With regard to developed countries, television has achieved a penetration level of 300 or more sets per 1,000 population in all developed countries. In those countries where penetration has surpassed the "300 point," the implementation of new technological developments—resulting from changes in regulation—has led to new usage patterns for the medium.

With regard to developing nations, penetration is increasing in the newly industrialized countries such as Brazil and South Korea, which would seem to be following a similar diffusion pattern to that evidenced in developed countries. In other developing nations such as Nigeria and Algeria, diffusion seems to stagnate when the technology has achieved full penetration of the urban elite segment. This trend fully confirms what Frey had identified during the early 1970s. It would seem, then, that only the newly industrialized nations achieve diffusion levels beyond that of the wealthy strata of the population.

Analysis of the data shows that, despite the trend toward worldwide diffusion of television, growth patterns vary widely. In developed countries, increased adoption is linked to changes in regulation allowing for the implementation of complementary technologies (for example, cable). In developing countries, differing diffusion patterns are related not only to the regulatory framework (for example, import controls on equipment), but also to income per capita.

### Political Variables in the Diffusion of Television

The growth of mass communications systems tends to be explained by analyzing the diffusion of information technologies at the receiver end—that is the mass public—at the expense of understanding why and how information technologies are made available to providers or sources, for example, government-owned or privately-held television stations. The lack of analysis in this area is particularly series. Given that signal sources are completely separate from receivers, one could almost consider two diffusion processes occurring in parallel: among sources, and among receivers. In this section, we will analyze the diffusion of television broadcasting among government-owned stations in order to underscore the importance of political factors in driving diffusion of information technologies at the source.

According to the conventional explanations of media systems growth, development of communication systems—such as broadcasting or the press—is the result of the socioeconomic transformations associated with the modernization processes. For example, the growth of media systems has been linked to either the processes of modernization and literacy (Lerner 1958; Alker 1966; McCronne and Cnudde 1967) or urbanization, literacy, and economic growth (Schramm and Ruggels 1967). From the perspective of conventional trade theory, the diffusion of technology among users is directly linked to the demand arising from a higher standard of living. These socioeconomic explanations of media systems growth would imply high correlation coefficients between indicators of economic growth such as per capita income, and indicators of media systems growth, such as the number of receiver sets (radio and television, alike) or the circulation of newspapers. Table 6.6 shows that—for users—there is a strong relation between the structure of demand in each country and the adoption of information technologies among users.

However, when one refers to adoption of the technology by the providers at the source, the correlation coefficients are smaller. For that purpose, for each country in our sample we examined the GNP per capita at the time of the introduction of television technology.[3] As Figure 6.5 shows, there is no relation at all between the level of development of a given country and the time of introduction of television.

It appears that neither the conventional approach nor trade theory provide an adequate explanation for diffusion of television broadcasting among countries. Furthermore, neither approach explains the tendency among later adopters to start broadcasting television programs at far lower levels of social and economic modernization.

**Table 6.6**
**Correlation between GNP per Capita and Media Indicators (1980)**

| | | |
|---|---|---|
| **Newspaper circulation** (Copies Per 1,000 Population) | 0.599 | (95) |
| **Radio receivers** (Sets Per 1,000 Population) | 0.507 | (126) |
| **Television Receivers** | 0.717 | (110) |

*Note:* The number between parentheses indicates sample size.
*Source:* UNESCO (1982); analysis by the author.

**Figure 6.5**
**Adoption of Television vs. GNP per Capita**

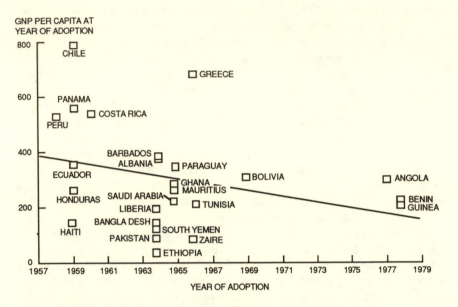

*Source:* UNESCO (1982); Katz and Weddell (1976). Analysis by the author.

We argue that the limitations of both theories relate to the absence of politi-cal variables. In fact, governments in the developing world are under pressure to provide certain services for their citizens, as soon as those services are implemented in other, more developed countries, and their citizens are knowledgeable of the availability of these services. Katz and Lefevre (1980) document several cases of African urban elites in the early 1960s pressuring their governments to establish television stations.

Another example of the importance of the political factor in international diffusion of information technologies is the fact that—despite the existence of multiple sources of a given technology—some countries systematically borrow from one source, while others borrow from a different one. In fact, qualitative evidence has shown that, in many cases, transfer of broadcasting technologies to developing countries was made by colonial powers

able to influence or even dictate the pattern of broadcasting in their dependent ter-ritories or in those countries over which they exercised some influence. (Katz and Wedell 1977, 65)

The authors explain that the transfer process took various forms, according to the nature of the relationship between the innovating country and the adopting nation:

Where there was a colonial relationship, the transfer of the metropolitan model was almost complete. Where there was no colonial relationship, the nature of the process of transfer was determined by economic, and perhaps political [reasons, such as] expansionism on the part of the developed country [or] dependence on the part of the developing state. (p. 68)

To illustrate this point we include a brief analysis regarding the diffusion of television technology among African countries.

The diffusion of television broadcasting technology among African countries was highly influenced by a complex blend of nationalistic and prestige-seeking communication policies, and the political processes and negotiations involved in the selection of a color television standard in Europe in the 1960s (Crane 1978). The inauguration of television broadcasting in the British colonies coincided in large measure with independence. In some countries, television was introduced after independence for overtly political reasons (Katz 1980). For example, in Nigeria, television was introduced in 1959 by the Eastern Region government so that the regional government could have a channel of expression independent from the federal Nigerian Broadcasting Corporation. In Ghana, television was not established until 1965, with the objective of "assisting in the social transformation of Ghana and [fighting] against neo-colonialism and imperialism."[4]

While this nationalistic tendency also existed in the former French colonies, France's strategy in marketing the French standard for television broadcasting also played a considerable role in the multiplication of systems in Africa. With the exception of Algerian TV—inaugurated in 1956 as an extension of French services—no Francophone African country implemented a television broadcasting system until 1962. However, between 1962 and 1967, ten former French colonies inaugurated indigenous services (see Table 6.7).

Within those ten systems, eight were built as a direct result of France's promotion of the SECAM standard. The decision of the French government to promote the SECAM color system (as opposed to PAL and NTSC) stemmed from the fact that SECAM was a French-owned technology (Crane 1978). As Crane puts it,

An anticipated economic return of billions of dollars from worldwide sales of the license rights for SECAM, professional and consumer electronics, as well as the possible sales of French color television programs, made the system a lucrative venture. (Crane 1978, 270)

It is important to mention that most of the systems did not broadcast in color until the early 1970s. Yet, their production equipment was all set up to SECAM standards.

France's general policy of promoting its technology was to offer parts of the system as gifts and then sell the remainder. For example, Gabon and the Ivory Coast were both given their first TV studios.

**Table 6.7**
**Diffusion of Television Technology in African Countries (1956–1980)**

| | FORMER ENGLISH COLONIES | | FORMER FRENCH COLONIES | | FORMER BELGIAN COLONIES | | PORTUGUESE COLONIES | |
|---|---|---|---|---|---|---|---|---|
| | N | % | N | % | N | % | N | % |
| 1956-1957 | 0 | 0 | 1 | 4.8 | 0 | 0 | 0 | 0 |
| 1958-1959 | 1 | 6.2 | 1 | 4.8 | 0 | 0 | 0 | 0 |
| 1960-1961 | 3 | 18.7 | 1 | 4.8 | 0 | 0 | 0 | 0 |
| 1962-1963 | 7 | 43.7 | 6 | 28.6 | 0 | 0 | 0 | 0 |
| 1964-1965 | 9 | 56.2 | 7 | 33.3 | 1 | 33.0 | 0 | 0 |
| 1966-1967 | 9 | 56.2 | 11 | 52.4 | 1 | 33.3 | 0 | 0 |
| 1968-1969 | 9 | 56.2 | 11 | 52.4 | 1 | 33.3 | 0 | 0 |
| 1970-1971 | 9 | 56.2 | 11 | 52.4 | 1 | 33.3 | 0 | 0 |
| 1972-1973 | 9 | 56.2 | 12 | 57.1 | 1 | 33.3 | 1 | 33.3 |
| 1974-1975 | 9 | 56.2 | 13 | 62.0 | 1 | 33.3 | 1 | 33.3 |
| 1976-1977 | 9 | 56.2 | 13 | 62.0 | 1 | 33.3 | 1 | 33.3 |
| 1978-1979 | 9 | 56.2 | 15 | 71.4 | 1 | 33.3 | 1 | 33.3 |
| Non-adopters | 7 | 43.7 | 6 | 28.6 | 2 | 66.6 | 2 | 66.6 |

*Source:* Katz (1985).

The following countries installed SECAM TV systems between 1962 and 1967: Congo (1962), Gabon (1963), Ivory Coast (1963), Madagascar (1967), Morocco (1962), Tunisia (1966), Zaire (1966), and Niger (1967). Senegal converted black-and-white systems to SECAM later.

In other African countries that were not colonialized by either England or France, politics played also a key role in adoption of television. For example, Ethiopia—one of the poorest countries in terms of GNP—has television, primarily because it was needed as part of the furnishings to make Addis Ababa a suitable setting for the Organization of African Unity (OAU) headquarters.

Therefore, the introduction of television broadcasting during the 1960s in Africa was largely the result of three factors: (1) the search for national prestige; (2) the satisfaction of urban elites' needs; and (3) the promotion of the SECAM standard by the French government. The slowing-down trend observed in the 1970s might be considered a result of the fact that a large percentage—41.7— of the former British colonies are nonadopters. The higher adoption rate of former French colonies may be related to the successful marketing efforts of the French in influencing government policy.

As the case has shown, historical influences continue to affect the media diffusion, as a result of the differing experiences arising from divergent colonial policies.

At this point we have concluded presenting the evidence of government intervention in the process of diffusion of information technologies. The general conclusion will summarize the results of the study and analyze them within the context of the overall argument.

## NOTES

1. Dates were obtained from sources quoted in Appendix 2, Table 2.1 of the UNESCO 1982 report.

2. Oceania was excluded from the graph, because of the reduced number of units.

3. See Collier and Messick (1975) for a similar approach to studying diffusion of social security policies among countries.

4. Declarations by President Nkrumah quoted in "Television," *West Africa,* June 3, 1965, p. 3.

# GENERAL CONCLUSION

In terms of their informational nature, societies can be characterized according to four types of indicators:

1. *information workers*—the information workers' share of the economically active population, as well as the industry breakdown of the information workforce;
2. *information technologies*—the level of diffusion of information technologies and the way they combine and substitute in order to support the society's flow of information;
3. *information flows*—the amount of information flowing through formal (measurable) and informal (nonmeasurable) channels; and
4. *information industries*—the contribution of the primary and secondary information industries to the GDP.

This study has dealt mainly with the first two indicators. In our concluding discussion, we first review the findings in each of the two main areas of analysis: workforce structure (Part I), and information technologies (Part II). Both analyses are viewed in the context of the overall argument, which reaffirms the importance of the political variable in determining the emergence of an information society. Then, the potential implications of these findings for developing countries' policymakers are explored. Finally, an agenda for guiding future research efforts around these issues is defined.

## EMERGENCE OF AN INFORMATION WORKFORCE

Chapter 1 showed that there is a uniform growth of information intensive occupations not only throughout the developed world, but also in most developing countries. In addition, it showed that the pattern of emergence of the information workforce differs widely according to each country. While several developing countries exhibit declining agricultural and rising industrial, service, and informational occupations, other developing countries have expanding information workforce combined with a stagnating or declining industrial workforce.

What are the causes for these different patterns of information sector growth? Chapter 2 showed that, in general, it is the state that fosters the expansion of the information workforce in the first stages of development—especially until the processes of industrialization and specialization become the leading independent variables. In general, while developed and newly-industrializing countries tend to allocate major portions of their information workforce to the manufacturing sector, many developing countries—particularly at lower levels of growth—tend to concentrate a major part of its information workers in the government sector. In this first stage, thus, information workforce growth is the result of the expansion of the government bureaucracy, as well as the demand for professionals and teachers—which is fostered by governmental support of basic services. This process is magnified by the expanding role of the state in developing countries' economies.

In addition, the high share of information occupations in the developing world is also the result of an increase in the supply of labor, due to population pressure—as well as the oversupply of an educated labor force by a dysfunctional education system. Within this context of oversupply of information workers, the government acts as a compensating mechanism at two levels. First, state and local government in developing countries will tend to grow in order to partially counter the rural-urban migration. Second, the central government will tend to grow beyond its needs, in order to absorb the increased supply of information workers.

It was also suggested in Chapter 2 that the growth of the information sector in the developing world is not uniform, but can accelerate or decelerate due to political factors. Authoritarian regimes, which can better control the social demands emerging from a context of unemployed information workers, will tend less to utilize the state as a mechanism of absorption of the unemployed information workforce. Conversely, democratic regimes in developing countries will tend to utilize the government as a means of hiring information workers—beyond what is rationally needed to manage public resources. Under these circumstances, democratic regimes in the developing world create more favorable conditions for the expansion of state bureaucracies and, therefore, growth of the information workforce.

## INTERNATIONAL DIFFUSION OF
## INFORMATION TECHNOLOGIES

Our main argument in Part II was that societies tend to adopt information technologies not only on the basis of technical feasibility or economic profitability, but also in terms of their political desirability.

After extensively reviewing the literature on diffusion of information technologies, Chapter 3 concluded that most of the recent theories that have been put forward to explain the interaction between information, communications, and society have focused almost exclusively on economic and social variables—excluding the political ones. Yet, the influence of political factors was implicit in most of these explanations. In addition, we pointed out that a phenomenon as pervasive as the expansion of the state and its influence on the diffusion of information technologies had been only superficially explored.

Based on this finding, we defined a historical model aimed at explaining the causes of diffusion of information technologies. According to this model, diffusion of information technologies is a process contingent on economic, social, and political variables. The importance of each of these variables changes according to different historical epochs. In the first stage of political development—that of state-building—it is the political variable that closely controls the diffusion process. For example, new states typically keep a strict control over the diffusion of mass communications technologies—allowing the diffusion of only those that either serve the purpose of creating a sense of national identity within societies often composed of disparate ethnic elements, or else support the political control of territories and populations. Since, at this stage, the political variable is most important in influencing diffusion of information technologies, the networks of international influence are key in determining the introduction of technologies in a given country.

In the second developmental stage, the economic variable gains weight, and information technologies are needed as part of each country's infrastructure for supporting economic growth. Yet, even at this stage, the political system may act as a constraint—by means of the regulatory process—on the satisfaction of information needs emerging from the economy.

In the third developmental stage—maturity—a new factor challenges the hegemony of the political variable. The private sector becomes the main consumer of communication and information systems, and tends to develop a conflictive relationship with the regulatory structures of the state. Parallel with this trend, technological developments that occurred in past years have led to a decrease in the price of equipment. This decrease in the price of message production devices limits the government's capability to enforce the control of diffusion of technologies. New media policies in France and Italy allowing for the installation of private radio stations, and legislation in Mexico authorizing the installation of satellite antennae for receiving television programs from U.S. cable and broadcasting networks are two examples of regulatory frameworks that have been obliged to adapt to challenges coming from the private sector. In conclusion, the stage of maturity is associated with a decline in importance of the political variable, and an increase in relevance of economic factors in determining diffusion of information technologies.

Having exposed the general model underlying Part II of the study, Chapters 4, 5, and 6 presented various types of evidence supporting our main argument. Chapter 4 showed how tariff policies have a decisive impact on the process of substitution between point-to-point communications technologies. We argue that an information technology does not diffuse in a vacuum, but is introduced within an environment—or communications ecosystem—where similar technologies are already widely utilized. When a new technology is introduced into the communications ecosystem, other cost-ineffective or less attractive substitutes can decline. Further, new relations of complementarity between old and new technologies can be created. Chapter 4 showed that, in fact, technological substitution or complementarity is a complex process not only driven by economic variables, but also shaped by policy and regulatory interventions.

Our evidence is twofold: first it was shown—using U.S. data—that replacement of first-class mail by the telephone was driven by the increase in postal rates, relative to telephone rates. Despite the fact that demand for first-class mail is quite inelastic, repeated rate increases render demand more elastic, and cross-elasticities between demand for mail and telephone develop. This is a typical case where the government controls the process of substitution—or traffic diversion—by a price mechanism.

The second area of evidence in Chapter 4 was of a more qualitative nature. Using secondary sources, the study shows that the diffusion of the telephone in Europe was partially affected by political determinants. The diffusion of telecommunications in Europe has been no random or single market-driven process. On the contrary, it has continually been constrained and/or driven forward through deliberate government policy decisions.

Finally, Chapter 4 showed that the decline of the telegraph in the developing world (as well as Europe and Japan) seems to be a much slower process than the one experienced in the United States. In the developing world, this situation is generally due to the fact that the government—which also controls the telephone agency—assumes a typically risk-averting behavior with regard to the introduction of new technology. If the government were to rapidly develop a long-distance network, this would cause capital losses in the telegraph system—also a state-operated entity. The slow development of a telephone network—while basically due to lack of capital—has the net effect of protecting the telegraph investment.

Having provided diverse examples of how politics influence the diffusion of technologies operated by the government, we then turned to explore the impact of the political factor on diffusion of technologies among private users. Chapter 5 illustrated the impact of a developing country's government policy on the rate of diffusion of computing within a given country. In Brazil, our case study, control of the diffusion of computers was implemented both by raising the barriers to entry of foreign firms and by raising the cost of equipment, as a result of import substitution policies. The net effect of this measure was a slowing in the country's rate of computerization. The choice of computing enabled us to prove that not only can governments control the diffusion of technologies they operate themselves, but they can also regulate the diffusion of information technologies among private users.

Finally, the importance of the political variable was also underscored in the analysis of international diffusion of information technologies among governments. Chapter 6 showed how conventional patterns of interaction between international trade and technological innovation—as presented by classical trade theory—can be affected by political factors. As shown in the case study of worldwide diffusion of television broadcasting, governments can control the rate of technological innovation. In many cases, the final goal in these actions can be characterized as being non-economic—that is, other than maximizing national income. Protection of industries that have heavy social implications, self-sufficiency, national security, and government control of information flow are some of the non-economic arguments justifying government intervention in the process of technological diffusion.

Data presented in Chapter 6 show that, despite the massive diffusion of electronic-based information technologies on a worldwide basis, the intracountry diffusion patterns of information technologies vary widely. Adoption of television by either public or private signal suppliers is an almost universal phenomenon. However, diffusion of this technology within each country follows different paths and is subject to different influences.

In developed countries, increased diffusion is linked to regulation changes allowing for the implementation of complementary technologies—such as cable TV—which permit them to surmount initial saturation levels. In developing countries, differing diffusion patterns are related not only to the regulatory factor, but also to the domestic structure of demand. Indeed, the domestic market still plays an important role in determining adoption of the technology. Despite the fact that the political variable was the main determinant behind the introduction of the technology into the country, it was not able to change the intracountry structure of demand. As a result, television in many developing countries only diffused within urban elites.

In sum, Part II showed three areas in which the political variable affects diffusion of information technologies: First, governments can—to a certain extent—control the introduction of a given technology into the territory. Second, regulatory policy can control the supply of information products and/or services. Third, access to the service and the reception of media signals is also constrained by policy decisions.

In addition, the study identified the mechanisms by which this influence is enacted. First, regulation can act to control access to the source of supply of media signals—therefore restricting the diffusion of receivers. Second, policymakers can restrict access to the media receiving equipment or computers, by means of implementing import controls. Third, import substitution policies that affect the pricing structure of hardware can greatly delay the computerization of local firms. Finally, by controlling the telecommunications agency, the government can automatically control the supply of services to the population.

From a theoretical perspective, it was argued that the reasons for government intervention vary widely, and can be related to a historical framework—

according to which the influence of the state on diffusion of information technologies is key at lower levels of economic and political development, and tends to dilute in postindustrial stages.

Is this state of affairs permanent? What are the major trends with regard to political intervention in the control of transition to informational stages of development? This study has shown that political intervention is the key variable in the first stages of development of both an information workforce and an information infrastructure. However, as industrialization progresses, it is the private sector that takes the lead in determining demand for information workers and explaining diffusion of information technologies.

It should be made clear, however, that the redefinition of the role of the state in the information field will not mean a complete withdrawal of governments from the field of information technology. The trend combines a tendency toward privatization of information goods production and delivery of service— as well as a strict control by the state of variables such as market access, imports, and spectrum allocation.

In conclusion, the role of the state will still remain key with regard to the transition toward an information society. We are witnessing a redefinition of the state's means of intervention—where the main examples are control of market access, regulation of the electromagnetic spectrum allocation process, and industrial policy in its larger sense.

Will developing countries ever follow the example of some industrialized nations, and deregulate their information industries? Even if privatization progresses in the developing world, the chances are that governments will continue to control the main aspects of the diffusion of information technologies, and, therefore, continue to catalyze the impact of market variables in the transition paths toward postindustrial stages.

## POLICY AND STRATEGIC IMPLICATIONS FOR DEVELOPING COUNTRIES

The information sector of the economy consists of capital (information technologies), as well as labor (information workers). The growth in the number of information workers is generally driven by the need to control, coordinate, and organize increasingly complex production processes. Diffusion of information technologies—namely, telecommunications and computers—is related to the need to increase productivity of information workers, as measured by their capability to process and transmit information. While the number of information workers has been growing consistently on a worldwide basis, the investment in information technologies—particularly in the developing world—is lagging. This situation has many implications both in terms of developing countries' government policies and the business strategies of information technology suppliers.

Part I shows that the information sector in most developing countries is growing faster than the manufacturing workforce. The causes of these trends are mainly three: (1) the substitution of information for noninformation labor in the manufacturing sector: (2) the changing internal composition within the service sector from personal services to social and distributive services; and (3) the expansion of governments.

The evidence also indicates a clear difference in the factors driving the growth of the information sector in developed and developing countries. In developed countries, information sector growth is mainly driven by the need to optimize and rationalize production processes. In developing countries, a large information sector is often an indication of economic inefficiency. Indeed, a large portion of information workers do not contribute to the management of industrial production processes, but are employed by domestic governments— which end up growing beyond their needs, in order to absorb the excess supply of information labor.

The oversupply of information workers in developing countries can be transformed into a driving force for development strategies. Government policymakers in the developing world can utilize this situation to their countries' advantage.

In general terms, policies should be implemented to adjust the supply and demand of information workers. In the educational field, further realignment between training policies and development objectives is required to prevent nonproductive employment of information workers. In the field of information technologies, the accelerated introduction of computers and communication services can help to control the growth of the information workforce, by fostering sector productivity. Finally, in the domain of industrial policy, the development of industries employing a high share of information workers should be promoted. Recommendations in the areas of information and industrial policies are discussed in more detail below.

Developing countries are lagging in the diffusion of information technologies. By fostering accelerated diffusion of carefully selected information technologies, policymakers can limit the inefficient employment of information workers. Information technologies can facilitate the management of decentralized organizational structures by supporting a more rapid and accurate feedback on performance and organizational processes, and can also help simplify management of the more complex new industries. Information technologies enable managers to have greater and more efficient control of production processes without decentralizing decision making. In turn, a centralization of decision-making process would result in less demand for information workers, thus reducing inefficient employment.

In the field of industrial policy, developing countries should encourage the development of industries that can efficiently employ a high share of information workers (such as on-line data bases, software, and data services). The oversupply of information workers can be converted into one of the main drivers of competitive advantage in certain information industries. Policymakers must define a policy in the information field, after deciding what position they want their countries to occupy in the value-added stream. Do they want their nations to be information creators or information processors? What is the appropriate mix of industries?

The labor structure and export opportunities of information service industries vary across industries. Given the increasing export opportunities in the information industries, some countries are exploiting their low salaries to become offshore data-entry centers, while others also aim at developing an export-oriented software industry. However, these types of initiative are still very limited. Few developing countries have defined industrial policies focusing on information-intensive industries.

In contrast, many developing countries have defined a hardware-driven information industrial policy. In fact, policymakers in the developing world are more often concerned about implementing policies aimed at producing information technology equipment, and less worried about optimizing its usage for increasing the productivity of the information sector and of the economy as a whole.

In many cases, information technology policies adopted by developing countries can have unforeseen impacts. For instance, an import substitution policy in the computer/telecommunications area can have a positive impact on the country's technological autarky, but a negative effect on its industrial infrastructure (in terms of limited diffusion of technology, and premature technological obsolescence). Information technology policies in developing countries have to be defined based on an in-depth understanding of the end users of those technologies.

## FUTURE RESEARCH DIRECTIONS IN THE
## POLITICAL ECONOMY OF THE INFORMATION SOCIETY

As expressed in Chapters 1 and 3, research on the international dimensions of the information society has only scratched the surface, in terms of both measuring and explaining the massive social and technological transformations that both developed and developing countries are undergoing. Two areas of research are particularly important to cover. First, measurements and analysis of the information workforce in developing countries remain discouragingly scarce. It is urgent to start developing case studies on specific countries.[1]

It is also important to pursue the analysis of the impact of information technologies on the performance of economic and political systems. In this area, studies on the macro impact of computing lag behind the work that has been done in the area of telecommunications and mass media. Finally, it is also urgent to start analyzing information flows in developing-country settings—following the pioneering efforts of Tomita (1975) and Pool et al. (1984).

To explain ongoing trends, it is important to analyze in detail the impact of political variables on the transition of information-intensive societies. This has to be done at two levels: First, it is important to analyze political structures as information-processing entities that generate demand for both information workers and information technologies.[2] Second, it is important to analyze the influence of policymaking processes on the deployment of information technologies.[3]

The concept of "information society"—developed for industrialized countries—is only an analytical benchmark against which different countries can be analyzed, rather than a model that nations must follow in order to enter postindustrial stages. As this study shows, there are as many profiles of an information society as there are countries in the world. It is suprising to find that a phenomenon as pervasive and varied as that of the emergence of information societies has not generated more research. We hope that, by answering some questions and raising more, this study serves as an impetus for further research.

## NOTES

1. See Jussawalla and Chee-Wah-Cheah (1982); and Jussawalla (1982).
2. See Deutsch (1963).
3. See Evans (1985).

# Appendix A:
# Alternative Approaches for
# Measuring the Size of
# the Information Workforce

In order to extend the comparative analysis of information workforce growth, it is necessary to generate cross-sectional time series. The production of census-based statistics in a volume appropriate to formulate cross-national comparisons requires an effort beyond the scope of this study. Instead, a set of measurements that provides a moderately reliable tool for estimating the size of the information workforce is defined and tested in this appendix.

The data base that was utilized is the *Yearbook of Labour Statistics* published annually by the International Labor Organization. Table 2B of the yearbook provides data on the distribution of the economically active population, in total and by sex, as well as by occupation according to the nine major groups of the 1968 International Standard Classification of Occupations (ISCO). In its editions of 1980 to the present, the yearbook also provides in Table 2C the same data cross-tabulated by industry.

Using as a starting point the inventory of information occupations defined by the OECD (see Chapter 1), it was assumed that Groups 1, 2, and 3 of the ISCO classification were composed exclusively of information workers:

*Information Sector*
1. Professional, technical and related workers
2. Administrative, executive, and managerial
3. Clerical

*Agriculture*
1. Farmers, fishermen, hunters

*Industry*
1. Miners, quarrymen, and related

2. Craftsmen, production process workers

*Service*

1. Workers in transport and communication

2. Sales workers

3. Service, sport, and recreation workers

4. Members of armed forces

The main disadvantage of this classification is, of course, the exclusion of tele-communication workers and media workers from the "information" category; they are included in the service category. Table A.1 presents all occupations that are considered information-based by the OECD inventory but are not included in the ISCO Groups 1, 2, and 3.

**Table A.1**
**Information-Intensive Occupations Not Included in ISCO Groups 1, 2, and 3**

I.   Information Producers

     Market search and coordination specialists

     4-10.20   Commodity brokers

     4-22      Purchasing agents and buyers

     4-31      Technical salesmen and advisers

     4-41      Insurance and stock agents, brokers and
               jobbers

     4-43.20   Auctioneers

II.  Information Gatherers

     4-43.30   Valuation surveyors

     7-54.70   Fabrics examiners

     8-59.20   Inspectors, viewers, and testers

     9-49.80   Quality inspectors

     5-89.20   Private inquiry agents

III. Information Processors

     Administration and managerial

     4-00      Managers (wholesale/retail trade)

               Process control and supervisory

     4-21      Sales supervisors

     5-20      Housekeeper

     5-31.20   Head cook

```
        6-00.30    Supervisors: clerical, sales, and other

        6-32.30    Forest supervisors

        7-0        Supervisors and general foremen (production)
IV.     Information Infrastucture Occupations

        Information machine workers

        8-49.65    Office machine repairmen

        8.62       Sound and vision equipment operators

        9-21       Compositors and typesetters

        9-22       Printing pressmen (except 9-22.70)

        9-23       Stereotypes and electrotypers

        9-24       Printing engravers (except 9-24.15 and
                   9-24.30)

        9-25       Photoengravers

        9-26       Bookbinders and related

        9-27       Photographic processors
Postal  and telecommunications

        8-54       Radio and television repairmen

        8-56       Telephone and telegraph installer/repairmen

        8-57.40    Telephone and telegraph linesmen

        8-62       Broadcasting station operators
```

The category of information infrastructure occupations is the one that is more seriously understated in the classification shown in Table A.2. In order to measure the total impact that this exclusion would have in measuring the information sector, we compared figures calculated using a highly disaggregated approach, such as Porat's (1977), with the figures obtained by simply aggregating the ISCO Groups 1, 2, and 3. Table A.2 and Figure A.1 present the results of this comparison for U.S. data.

The comparison reveals an overall good fit of both series, with the exception of an underestimation for the "aggregated" series for 1960 and 1970. The difference in trends can be due to the fact that the 1980 data point for the Porat series was an estimate generated in 1978, but the 1980 figure for the aggregated series was obtained from 1980 Census data (U.S. Department of Commerce, 1984).

**Table A.2**
**Comparative Measurements of the U.S. Workforce Structure***

| | 1900 | 1910 | 1920 | 1930 | 1940 | 1950 | 1960 | 1970 | 1980 |
|---|---|---|---|---|---|---|---|---|---|
| *Aggregated approach* | | | | | | | | | |
| Information | 3,808 | 6,207 | 8,471 | 11,261 | 12,631 | 17,228 | 22,442 | 32,232 | 45,579 |
| Professional, technical | 1,234 | 1,758 | 2,283 | 3,311 | 3,879 | 5,000 | 7,336 | 11,561 | 15,968 |
| Managers, officials | 1,697 | 2,462 | 2,803 | 3,614 | 3,770 | 5,096 | 5,489 | 6,463 | 11,138 |
| Clerical | 877 | 1,987 | 3,385 | 4,336 | 4,982 | 7,132 | 9,617 | 14,208 | 18,473 |
| Agriculture | 10,888 | 11,533 | 11,390 | 10,322 | 8,994 | 6,858 | 4,086 | 2,450 | 2,741 |
| Farmers and farm managers | 5,763 | 6,163 | 6,442 | 6,032 | 5,362 | 4,325 | 2,526 | 1,428 | |
| Farm laborers | 5,125 | 5,370 | 4,948 | 4,290 | 3,632 | 2,533 | 1,560 | 1,022 | |
| Industry | 10,402 | 14,234 | 16,974 | 19,272 | 20,596 | 23,733 | 25,617 | 29,168 | 26,883 |
| Craftsmen, foremen | 3,062 | 4,315 | 5,482 | 6,246 | 6,203 | 8,205 | 9,241 | 11,082 | 12,787 |
| Operatives | 3,720 | 5,441 | 6,587 | 7,691 | 9,518 | 11,754 | 12,846 | 14,335 | 10,565 |
| Laborers | 3,620 | 4,478 | 4,905 | 5,335 | 4,875 | 3,774 | 3,530 | 3,751 | 3,531 |
| Service | 3,933 | 5,317 | 5,370 | 7,831 | 9,519 | 10,041 | 12,391 | 15,876 | 13,228 |
| Private household workers | 1,579 | 1,851 | 1,411 | 1,998 | 2,412 | 1,492 | 1,825 | 1,204 | |
| Service workers | 1,047 | 1,711 | 1,901 | 2,774 | 3,657 | 4,524 | 5,765 | 9,047 | |
| Salesworkers | 1,307 | 1,755 | 2,058 | 3,059 | 3,450 | 4,025 | 4,801 | 5,625 | |
| Total | 29,031 | 37,291 | 42,205 | 48,686 | 51,740 | 57,860 | 64,536 | 79,726 | 88,431 |
| Information (%) | 13.1 | 16.6 | 20.1 | 23.1 | 24.4 | 29.8 | 34.8 | 40.4 | 51.5 |
| Agriculture (%) | 37.5 | 30.9 | 27.0 | 21.2 | 17.4 | 11.9 | 6.3 | 3.1 | 3.1 |
| Industry (%) | 35.8 | 38.2 | 40.2 | 39.6 | 39.8 | 41.0 | 39.7 | 36.6 | 30.4 |
| Service (%) | 13.5 | 14.3 | 12.7 | 16.1 | 18.4 | 17.4 | 19.2 | 19.9 | 15.0 |
| *Porat (1976)* | | | | | | | | | |
| Information (%) | 12.8 | 14.9 | 17.7 | 24.5 | 24.9 | 30.8 | 42.0 | 46.4 | 46.6 |
| Agriculture (%) | 35.3 | 31.1 | 32.5 | 20.4 | 15.4 | 11.9 | 6.0 | 3.1 | 2.1 |
| Industry (%) | 26.8 | 36.3 | 32.0 | 35.3 | 37.2 | 38.3 | 34.8 | 28.6 | 22.5 |
| Services (%) | 25.1 | 17.7 | 17.8 | 19.8 | 22.5 | 19.0 | 17.2 | 21.9 | 28.8 |

*Sources:* U.S. Historical Statistics, p. 139; U.S. Department of Commerce (1984), p. 417; Porat (1976).
*In thousands, except where percent is indicated.

**Figure A.1**
**Information Sector Growth in the United States,**
**Aggregated Measurement versus Porat (1975; 1976), 1900–80**

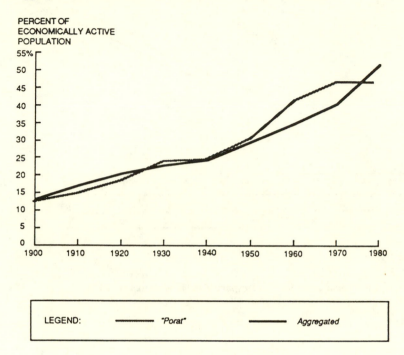

PERCENT OF
ECONOMICALLY ACTIVE
POPULATION

LEGEND: ———————— "Porat"  ———————— Aggregated

In order to further check this approach for measuring the information sector, we compared our data for the British workforce structure with that provided by OECD (1981) and Wall (1977) (Figure A.2).

In the first place, Figure A.2 shows that the series based on two data points obtained by aggregating ISCO Groups 1, 2, and 3 reveals an underestimation of the information sector, which is particularly serious for 1966 (approximately 8 percent smaller than Wall's and 6 percent smaller than OECD's). However, this underestimation tends to decrease in 1970, when the difference is only 2 percent.

Figure A.3 shows a comparison of the total workforce structure according to the three sources for 1970. It shows that the analysis of the workforce structure according to a four-sector aggregation scheme can be properly done by using one-digit occupational categories. The only variation between the aggregated estimation and the two others resides in the underestimation of the service sector and the consequent overestimation of the size of the industrial sector. The main reason for this variation is that the aggregated statistics provided by the ILO Yearbook included workers in transportation within the industrial sector and did not include them in the service sector, where they belong.

**Figure A.2**
**Information-Sector Growth in the United Kingdom,**
**Comparative Measurements, 1900–70**

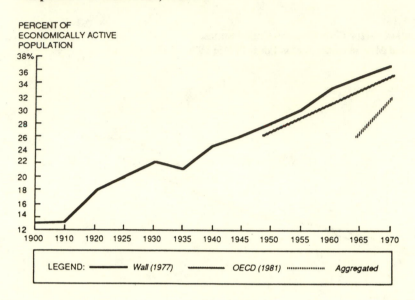

PERCENT OF
ECONOMICALLY ACTIVE
POPULATION

LEGEND: ———— Wall (1977)   ••••••••• OECD (1981)   ................ Aggregated

**Figure A.3**
**Structure of the British Workforce, Comparative Measurements, 1970**

PERCENT OF
ECONOMICALLY ACTIVE
POPULATION

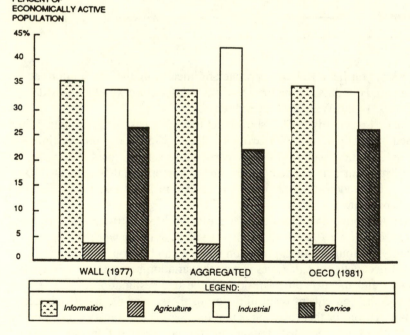

LEGEND:

Information   Agriculture   Industrial   Service

**Figure A.4**
**Information Sector Estimates in Variance,**
**Disaggregated Minus Aggregated Measures**

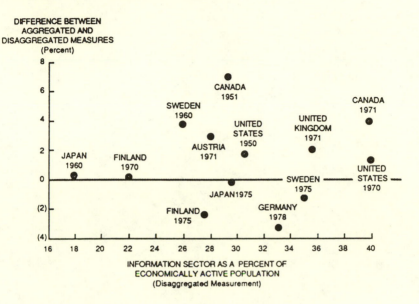

DIFFERENCE BETWEEN
AGGREGATED AND
DISAGGREGATED MEASURES
(Percent)

INFORMATION SECTOR AS A PERCENT OF
ECONOMICALLY ACTIVE POPULATION
(Disaggregated Measurement)

In order to complete our reliability check of the proposed measures of the information workforce, we have calculated the difference in percentage points between the disaggregated measurement "a la Porat" and the aggregation of ISCO occupational categories 1, 2, and 3.

Data presented in Figure A.4 show that, with the exception of Canada for 1951, the aggregated measurement provides a confidence interval of ±4 percent.

This difference leads us to the conclusion that this methodology, if used prudently, can be utilized for estimating the size of the information sector for those countries for which we do not have disaggregated statistics. In addition, it constitutes an appropriate tool for producing cross-national comparisons of growth trends in the workforce structure.

# Appendix B:
# Time Series for Regression Analyses of Technological Substitution (Chapter 4)

| | Telephone Calls per Capita | Letters per Capita | GNP | Telephone Cost | Mail Tariff |
|---|---|---|---|---|---|
| | $(C_t/P_t)$ | $(L_t/P_t)$ | $(Y_t/P_t)$ | $(Tc_t)$ | $(Tl_t)$ |
| 1886 | 5.4 | 38.80 | 774 | 6.00 | 33 |
| 1887 | 6.3 | 35.41 | 774 | 6.00 | 33 |
| 1888 | 6.4 | 35.47 | 774 | 6.00 | 33 |
| 1889 | 7.4 | 37.49 | 795 | 5.80 | 33 |
| 1890 | 8.4 | 38.11 | 836 | 5.80 | 33 |
| 1891 | 9.2 | 40.74 | 856 | 5.80 | 33 |
| 1892 | 10.6 | 43.64 | 920 | 5.70 | 33 |
| 1893 | 10.4 | 44.99 | 859 | 5.70 | 33 |
| 1894 | 11.4 | 43.23 | 819 | 5.70 | 33 |
| 1895 | 13.5 | 44.27 | 900 | 5.70 | 33 |
| 1896 | 13.9 | 48.19 | 865 | 5.70 | 33 |
| 1897 | 16.0 | 48.05 | 930 | 5.60 | 33 |
| 1898 | 19.5 | 50.73 | 933 | 5.60 | 33 |
| 1899 | 25.9 | 52.75 | 1,000 | 5.60 | 33 |
| 1900 | 37.8 | 56.22 | 1,011 | 5.60 | 33 |
| 1901 | 52.1 | 57.42 | 1,105 | 5.60 | 33 |
| 1902 | 66.1 | 61.28 | 1,093 | 5.45 | 33 |
| 1903 | 70.5 | 66.13 | 1,126 | 5.45 | 33 |
| 1904 | 78.6 | 69.39 | 1,092 | 5.45 | 33 |
| 1905 | 94.4 | 72.92 | 1,149 | 5.45 | 33 |
| 1906 | 112.1 | 80.72 | 1,258 | 5.45 | 33 |
| 1907 | 124.9 | 84.51 | 1,255 | 5.45 | 33 |
| 1908 | 131.6 | 90.39 | 1,130 | 5.45 | 33 |
| 1909 | 136.1 | 92.86 | 1,290 | 5.45 | 33 |

| | Telephone Calls per Capita | Letters per Capita | GNP | Telephone Cost | Mail Tariff |
|---|---|---|---|---|---|
| | $(C_t/P_t)$ | $(L_t/P_t)$ | $(Y_t/P_t)$ | $(Tc_t)$ | $(Tl_t)$ |
| 1910 | 142.8 | 96.42 | 1,299 | 5.45 | 33 |
| 1911 | 148.4 | 108.03 | 1,313 | 5.45 | 33 |
| 1912 | 155.5 | 110.70 | 1,366 | 5.45 | 33 |
| 1913 | 153.8 | 114.58 | 1,351 | 5.45 | 33 |
| 1914 | 151.1 | 118.66 | 1,267 | 5.45 | 33 |
| 1915 | 162.7 | 120.22 | 1,238 | 5.45 | 33 |
| 1916 | 177.5 | 121.76 | 1,317 | 5.45 | 33 |
| 1917 | 183.6 | 123.56 | 1,310 | 5.00 | 50 |
| 1918 | 177.2 | 126.97 | 1,471 | 5.00 | 50 |
| 1919 | 170.7 | 128.78 | 1,401 | 4.65 | 33 |
| 1920 | 177.6 | 127.30 | 1,315 | 4.65 | 33 |
| 1921 | 180.8 | 125.71 | 1,177 | 4.65 | 33 |
| 1922 | 189.1 | 124.84 | 1,345 | 4.65 | 33 |
| 1923 | 200.9 | 123.57 | 1,482 | 4.65 | 33 |
| 1924 | 206.0 | 122.06 | 1,450 | 4.65 | 33 |
| 1925 | 212.1 | 126.02 | 1,549 | 4.65 | 33 |
| 1926 | 221.3 | 130.04 | 1,619 | 3.40 | 33 |
| 1927 | 225.9 | 136.80 | 1,594 | 3.25 | 33 |
| 1928 | 234.1 | 138.63 | 1,584 | 3.25 | 33 |
| 1929 | 247.7 | 141.47 | 1,671 | 3.00 | 33 |
| 1930 | 247.7 | 137.88 | 1,490 | 3.00 | 33 |
| 1931 | 242.8 | 128.28 | 1,364 | 3.00 | 33 |
| 1932 | 225.1 | 117.65 | 1,154 | 3.00 | 33 |
| 1933 | 209.3 | 87.10 | 1,126 | 3.00 | 50 |
| 1934 | 212.0 | 91.90 | 1,220 | 3.00 | 50 |
| 1935 | 218.3 | 98.92 | 1,331 | 3.00 | 50 |
| 1936 | 233.6 | 100.47 | 1,506 | 2.50 | 50 |
| 1937 | 245.0 | 109.06 | 1,576 | 2.20 | 50 |
| 1938 | 246.5 | 111.20 | 1,484 | 2.20 | 50 |
| 1939 | 257.4 | 113.68 | 1,598 | 2.20 | 50 |
| 1940 | 273.2 | 117.34 | 1,720 | 1.90 | 50 |
| 1941 | 286.0 | 122.54 | 1,977 | 1.75 | 50 |
| 1942 | 291.8 | 130.19 | 2,208 | 1.75 | 50 |
| 1943 | 289.0 | 145.39 | 2,465 | 1.75 | 50 |
| 1944 | 292.1 | 162.56 | 2,611 | 1.75 | 50 |
| 1945 | 308.5 | 165.19 | 2,538 | 1.75 | 50 |
| 1946 | 333.8 | 148.34 | 2,211 | 1.55 | 50 |
| 1947 | 354.8 | 149.44 | 2,150 | 1.55 | 50 |
| 1948 | 380.1 | 155.68 | 2,208 | 1.55 | 50 |
| 1949 | 394.3 | 161.85 | 2,172 | 1.55 | 50 |
| 1950 | 411.8 | 167.64 | 2,342 | 1.55 | 50 |
| 1951 | 418.8 | 173.97 | 2,485 | 1.55 | 50 |

|  | Telephone Calls per Capita | Letters per Capita | GNP | Telephone Cost | Mail Tariff |
|---|---|---|---|---|---|
|  | $(C_t/P_t)$ | $(L_t/P_t)$ | $(Y_t/P_t)$ | $(Tc_t)$ | $(Tl_t)$ |
| 1952 | 424.6 | 179.16 | 2,517 | 1.50 | 50 |
| 1953 | 448.0 | 181.29 | 2,587 | 1.50 | 50 |
| 1954 | 456.5 | 177.18 | 2,506 | 1.50 | 50 |
| 1955 | 473.2 | 183.68 | 2,650 | 1.50 | 50 |
| 1956 | 495.8 | 188.67 | 2,652 | 1.50 | 50 |
| 1957 | 513.3 | 193.95 | 2,642 | 1.50 | 50 |
| 1958 | 531.3 | 194.17 | 2,569 | 1.50 | 67 |
| 1959 | 557.7 | 190.83 | 2,688 | 1.45 | 67 |
| 1960 | 584.4 | 192.19 | 2,699 | 1.45 | 67 |
| 1961 | 590.7 | 195.32 | 2,706 | 1.45 | 67 |
| 1962 | 605.9 | 198.51 | 2,840 | 1.45 | 67 |
| 1963 | 620.1 | 198.31 | 2,912 | 1.45 | 83 |
| 1964 | 644.7 | 201.15 | 3,028 | 1.45 | 83 |
| 1965 | 680.6 | 205.13 | 3,180 | 1.40 | 83 |
| 1966 | 721.7 | 216.03 | 3,348 | 1.40 | 83 |
| 1967 | 755.8 | 223.39 | 3,398 | 1.40 | 83 |
| 1968 | 794.7 | 226.34 | 3,521 | 1.30 | 100 |
| 1969 | 842.1 | 238.69 | 3,580 | 1.30 | 100 |
| 1970 | 884.6 | 246.18 | 3,555 | 1.05 | 100 |

*Sources:*
- Telephone calls per capita:
  (Local calls + toll calls)/population
  Telephone calls include Bell and independent companies
- Letters per capita:
  (First class mail + domestic air mail)/population
- GNP:
  Gross National Product per capita at 1958 dollars
- Cost of telephone call:
  Real cost of a telephone call
- Cost of letter:
  Real letter tariff expressed in cents (index 1970 = 100)

(All statistics obtained from U.S. Department of Commerce, Bureau of the Census, 1975. *Historical Statistics of the United States, Colonial Times to 1970*. Washington, DC: U.S. Bureau of the Census.)

# Bibliography

Ahmed, S. 1984. *Public Finance in Egypt*. World Bank Staff Working Paper No. 639. Washington, D.C.: World Bank.

Akerlof, G. 1970. "The Market for 'Lemons': Quality Uncertainty and Market Mechanism," *Quarterly Journal of Economics* 84 (August):488–500.

Alchian, A. 1969. "Information Costs, Pricing and Resource Unemployment," *Journal of Western Economy* 7 (June):109–28.

Alker, H. 1966. "Causal Inferences and Political Analysis," Bernd, J. (ed.), *Mathematical Applications in Political Science*. Dallas: Southern Methodist Press.

Almond, G. A., and Powell, G. B., 1978. *Comparative Politics*. Boston: Little, Brown.

Anderson, K., and Baldwin, R. 1981. *The Political Market for Protection in Industrialized Countries: Empirical Evidence*. World Bank Staff Working Paper No. 492. Washington, D.C.: World Bank.

Apter, D. E. 1965. *The Politics of Modernization*. Chicago, IL: The University of Chicago Press.

Arrow, K. 1963. "Uncertainty and the Welfare Economics of Medical Care," *American Economic Review* 53 (December):941–73.

Attali, J., and Stourdze, Y. 1977. "The Birth of the Telephone and Economic Crisis: The Slow Death of the Monologue in French Society," in Pool, I. de Sola (ed.), *The Social Impact of the Telephone*. Cambridge, Mass.: The M.I.T. Press.

Bain, A. 1962. "The Growth of Television Ownership in the United Kingdom," *International Economic Review* 3:145–67.

Bairoch, P. (trans. by Lady Cynthia Postan). 1977. *The Economic Development of the Third World since 1900*. Berkeley: University of California Press. Excerpts reprinted by permission of the publisher and Methuen and Co. (London).

Barnes, J., and Lamberton, D. 1976. "The Growth of the Australian Information Society," quoted in Lamberton, D. "The Theoretical Implications of Measuring the Communications Sector," in Lamberton, D., and Jussawalla, M. (eds.), *Communication Economics and Development*. New York: Pergamon Press.

Barquin, R. 1974. *The Transfer of Computer Technology: A Framework for Policy in the Latin American Nations*. Unpublished Ph.D. thesis, Massachusetts Institute of Technology.

Bebee, E. L., and Gilling, E. T. W. 1976. "Telecommunications and Economics Development: A Model for Planning and Policy Making," *Telecommunications Journal* 43 (August):537–43.

Bell, D. 1973. *The Coming of Post-Industrial Society*. New York: Basic Books.

————. 1979. "The Social Framework of the Information Society," in Dertouzos, M., and Moses, J. (eds.), *The Computer Age: A Twenty-year View*. Cambridge, Mass. The M.I.T. Press.

Berelson, B., Lazarsfeld, P., and McPhee, W. 1954. *Voting*. Chicago: University of Chicago Press.

Bergensen, A., and Schoenberg, R. 1980. "Long Waves of Colonial Expansion and Contraction, 1415-1969," in Bergensen, A. (ed.), *Studies of the Modern World-System*. New York: Academic Press.

Bhagwati, J. 1971. "The Generalized Theory of Distortions and Welfare," in Bhagwati, J., *Trade, Balance of Payments and Growth*. Amsterdam: North Holland.

Bhalla, A. 1973. "A Disaggregative Approach to LDCs Tertiary Sector," *The Journal of Development Studies* 10:50-65.

Bird, R. 1971. "Wagner's 'Law' of Expanding State Activity," *Public Finance* 26:1-25.

Blades, D., Johnston, D., and Marcezewski, W. 1974. *Service Activities in Developing Countries*. Paris: OECD.

Brock, G. 1981. *The Telecommunications Industry*. Cambridge, Mass.: Harvard University Press.

Burlingame, R. 1961. "Information Technology and Decentralization," *Harvard Business Review* 39:121-26.

Cameron, D. 1978. "The Expansion of the Public Economy: A Comparative Analysis," *American Political Science Review* 72:1243-61.

Caves, R., and Holton, R. 1959. *The Canadian Economy*. Cambridge, Mass.: Harvard University Press.

CCITT. 1972. *Economic Studies at the National Level in the Field of Telecommunications, 1964-1972*. Study Group GAS-5, International Telephone and Telegraph Consultative Committee (CCITT): Geneva, ITU.

Chandler, R. 1977. *The Visible Hand*. Cambridge, Mass.: Harvard University Press.

Chow, G. 1967. "Technological Change and the Demand for Computers," *American Economic Review* 57.

Clark, C. 1957. *Conditions of Economic Progress*. London: Macmillan.

Claval, S. 1980. "Center/Periphery and Space: Models of Political Geography," in Gottman, J. (ed.), *Centre and Periphery: Spatial Variations in Politics*. Beverly Hills, Calif.: Sage.

Clippinger, J. 1976. *Who Gains by Communications Development? Studies of Information Technologies in Developing Countries*. Program on Information Technologies and Public Policy Working Paper No. 76-1, Harvard University, January.

Coleman, J., Katz, E., and Menzel, H. (1957). "Diffusion of An Innovation Among Physicians," *Sociometry*, 20:253-270.

Collier, D., and Messick R. 1975. "Prerequisites versus Diffusion: Testing Alternative Explanations of Social Security Adoption," *American Political Science Review* 69:1299-1315.

Collins, H. 1980. "Forecasting the Use of Innovative Telecommunications Services," *Futures* (April):106-12.

Crain, R. 1966. "Fluoridation: The Diffusion of an Innovation among Cities," *Social Forces* 44 (June):467–76.

Crane, R. 1978. "Communications Standards and the Politics of Protectionism," *Telecommunications Policy* (December).

Cruise O'Brien, R., Cooper, E., Perkes, B., and Lucas, H. 1977. *Communication Indicators and Indicators of Socio-Economic Development, 1960–1970.* Unpublished study, University of Sussex: Institute of Development Studies.

Cutright, P. 1963. "National Political Development: Measurement and Analysis," *American Sociological Review* 27 (April).

Dahrendorf, R. 1967. *Society and Democracy in Germany.* Garden City, N.Y.: Doubleday.

De Fleur, M. 1978. *Theories of Mass Communication* (first edition). New York: Longman.

De Fleur, M., and Ball-Rokeach, S. 1982. *Theories of Mass Communications.* New York: Longman.

De Leon, P. 1979. *Development and Diffusion of the Nuclear Power Reactor: A Comparative Analysis.* Cambridge, Mass.: Ballinger Publishing.

Deutsch, K. 1956. "Anatomy and Boundaries according to communications theory," in Roy Grinker (ed.), *Toward a Unified Theory of Human Behavior.* New York: Basic Books.

_____. 1957. *Nationalism and Socialism Communication.* Cambridge, Mass.: The M.I.T. Press. Excerpts reprinted with permission.

_____. 1963. *The Nerves of Government: Models of Political Communication and Control.* New York: Free Press.

_____. 1964. "Transaction Flows as Indicators of Political Cohesion," in Jacob, P., and Toscano, J. (eds.), *The Integration of Political Communities.* Philadelphia: University of Pennsylvania.

_____. 1967. "Nation and World," in Pool, I. de Sola (ed.), *Contemporary Political Science.* New York: McGraw-Hill.

Deutsch, K., and Isard, W. 1961. "A Note on a Generalized Concept of Effective Distance," *Behavior Science* 6 (October): 308–11.

Downs, G., and Mohr, L. 1976. "Conceptual Issues in the Study of Innovation," *Administrative Science Quarterly* 21:700–14.

Duch, R., and Lemieux, P. 1986. *The Political Economy of Communications Development.* Paper presented at the Annual Convention of the International Communications Association, Chicago, IL.

Durkheim, E. 1893. *De la division du travail social.* Paris: Alcan.

Evans, P. 1985. *State, Capital, and the Transformation of Dependence: The Brazilian Computer Case.* Working paper no. 6 on comparative development, Brown University.

Ewing, D., and Salaman, R. 1977. *The Postal Crisis: The Postal Function as a Communicative Service.* Office of Telecommunications Special Publication 77–13. Washington, D.C.: U.S. Department of Commerce.

Fisher, A. G. B. 1933. "Capital and the Growth of Knowledge," *Economic Journal*: 374–89.

Freeman, C. 1973. "The Plastics Industry: A Comparative Study of Research and Innovation," *National Institute of Economics Review* (November):22–26.

Frey, F. 1973. "Communications and Development," in Pool, I. de Sola (ed.), *Handbook of Communications.* Chicago: Rand McNally.

Fuchs, V. R. 1968. *The Service Economy*. New York: National Bureau of Economic Research.

Galbraith, K. 1968. *The New Industrial State*. Boston: Houghton Mifflin.

Garbade, K., and Silber, W. 1978. "Technology, Communication and the Performance of Financial Markets: 1840-1975," *The Journal of Finance* 33 (June):819-32.

Gemmel, N. 1982. "Economic Development and Structural Change: The Role of the Service Sector," *The Journal of Development Studies* 19:37-66.

Gerschenkron, A. 1952. "Economic Backwardness in Historical Perspective," in Hoselitz, B. (ed.), *The Progress of the Underdeveloped Countries*. Chicago: University of Chicago Press.

Gershuny, J. 1977. "Post-Industrial Society: The Myth of the Service Economy," *Futures* 9:103-14.

————. 1978. *After Industrial Society*. London: Macmillan.

Goffman, I., and Mahar, D. 1971. "The Growth of Public Expenditures in Selected Developing Nations: Six Caribbean Countries 1940-65," *Public Finance* 26:57-73.

Gottman, J. 1980. "Confronting Centre and Periphery," in Gottman, J. (ed.), *Centre and Periphery: Spatial Variations in Politics*. Beverly Hills, Calif.: Sage.

Gray, V. 1973. "Innovation in the States: A Diffusion Study," *American Political Science Review* 67:1174-85.

Griliches, Z. 1957. "Hybrid Corn: An Exploration In The Economics of Technological Change," *Econometrica*, 25:501-22.

Gronau, R. 1945. "Information and Frictional Unemployment," *American Economic Review* 35 (September):519-30.

Gupta, S. P. 1967. "Public Expenditures and Economic Growth: A Time-Series Analysis," *Public Finance* 22 (4):458.

Han, S. 1978. "Development de l'informatique en Yugoslavie," in UNESCO.

Hardy, A. 1980. *The Role of the Telephone in Economic Development*. Institute for Communications Research, Stanford University, January.

Heller, P., and Tait, A. 1983. *Government Employment and Pay: Some International Comparisons*. IMF: Fiscal Affairs Department, DM/83/29.

Heyer, P. 1981. "Innis and the History of Communications: Antecedents, Parallels and Unsuspected Biases," in Melody, W., et al., *Culture, Communication and Dependency: The Tradition of H. A. Innis*: Norwood, N.J.: Ablex.

Hirschman, A. 1982. *Shifting Involvements*. Princeton: Princeton University Press.

Hirschman, A. O. 1970. *Exit, Voice, and Loyalty: Responses to Decline in Firms, Organizations, and States*. Cambridge, MA: Harvard University Press.

Hobsbawn, E. J. 1969. *Industry and Empire*, Vol. 3 of *The Pelican History of Britain*. London: Penguin.

Hudson, H., Goldschmidt, D., Parker, E., and Hardy, A. 1979. *The Role of Telecommunications in Socioeconomic Development*. Keewatin Communication, mimeographed.

Hufbauer, G. 1966. *Synthetic Materials and the Theory of International Trade*. Cambridge, Mass.: Harvard University Press.

ILO (International Labor Organization). 1968. *Yearbook of Labour Statistics*. Geneva, Switzerland: International Labour Office.

ILO (International Labour Organization). 1983. *Yearbook of Labour Statistics*. Geneva: ILO.

Innis, H. 1923. *A History of the Canadian Pacific Railway*. London: P. S. King and Son.

————. 1950. *Empire and Communication*. Toronto: University of Toronto Press.

Irwin, M. 1981. "U.S. Telecommunications Regulation," *Telecommunications Policy*, March. London: 1PC Business Press, 28.

Jacob, P., and Teune, H. 1964. "The Integrative Process: Guidelines for Analysis of the Bases of Political Community," in Jacob, P., and Toscano, J. (eds.), *The Integration of Political Communities*. Philadelphia: University of Pennsylvania Press.

Jipp, A. 1963. "Wealth of Nations and Telephone Density," *Telecommunications Journal* (July):199–201.

Johnson, H. 1968. *Comparative Cost and Commercial Policy Theory for a Developing World Economy*. Stockholm: Almqwist and Wicksell.

Jonscher, C. 1981. *The Impact of Telecommunications on the Performance of a Sample of Business Enterprises in Kenya: A Research Report to the International Telecommunication Union*. New York: Communications Studies and Planning International, August.

————. 1982a. *Economic Causes of the Rising of Information-Intensive Societies*. Unpublished paper, Harvard University, February.

————. 1982b. *Productivity Change and the Growth of Information Processing Requirements in the Economy: Theory and Empirical Analysis*. Unpublished paper, Harvard University, February.

————. 1983. "Information Resources and Economic Productivity," *Information Economics and Policy* 1:13–35. Excerpts reprinted with permission of North-Holland Publishing (Amsterdam).

————. 1986. "Telecommunications Liberalization in the United Kingdom," in Snow, M. (ed.), *Marketplace for Telecommunications*. New York: Longman.

Jussawalla, M. 1980. "The Transfer of Communications Technology," *Telecommunications Policy* (December):249–62.

————. 1982. *The Future of the Information Economy*. Unpublished paper, East-West Center, Honolulu.

Jussawalla, M., and Chee-Wah-Cheah. 1982. *Towards an Information Economy: The Case of Singapore*. Unpublished manuscript, East-West Communication Institute, Honolulu, July.

Katouzian, M. 1970. "The Development of the Service Sector: A New Approach," *Oxford Economic Papers*, 22:362–82. Excerpt reprinted with permission of Oxford University Press.

Katz, E., and Lazarsfeld, P. 1955. *Personal Influence*. Glencoe, Ill.: Free Press.

Katz, E., and Wedell, G. 1977. *Broadcasting in the Third World*. London: Macmillan.

Katz, R. 1980. *Communications et Politiques de Coopération Bilatérale en Afrique Occidentale*. Unpublished thesis, University of Paris II.

————. 1981. *Nationalism and Computer Technology Transfer: The Case of Brazil*. Unpublished M.S. thesis, Massachusetts Institute of Technology.

————. 1984. *Política Nacional de Informática en India*. Report to the National Informatics Commission, Buenos Aires.

————. 1985. *An International Perspective on the Information Society*. Unpublished Ph.D. dissertation, Massachusetts Institute of Technology.

————. 1986a. "Explaining Information Sector Growth in Developing Countries," *Telecommunications Policy* 10 (September):209–28. Reprinted with permission of Butterworth & Co. (London).

_____. 1986b. "Measurement and Cross-National Comparisons of the Information Work Force," *The Information Society* 4 (December):231-77.

Katz, R., and Lefevre, B. 1980. *L'Etat des Communications dans les Pays Africains Francophones ou Utilisant la Langue Français*. Study prepared for UNESCO, Division of Free Flow of Information.

Keen, P., and Scott Morton, M. 1978. *Decision Support Systems: An Organizational Perspective*. Reading, Mass.: Addison-Wesley.

Kindleberger, C. P. 1969. *Foreign Trade and the National Economy*. New Haven: Yale University Press.

Kohl, J. 1983. "The Functional Structure of Public Expenditures: Long Term Changes," in Taylor, C. L. (ed.), *Why Governments Grow: Measuring Public Sector Size*. Beverly Hills, Calif.: Sage. Excerpts reprinted with permission.

Kollen, J., and Garwood, J. 1975. *Travel/Communications Tradeoffs: The Potential for Substitution among Business Travelers*. Headquarters Business Planning Group, Bell Canada, Montreal.

Kraus, S. and Davis, D. 1976. *The Effects Of Mass Communication On Political Behavior*. University Park, PA: The Pennsylvania State University Press.

Kusnetz, S. 1957. "Quantitative Aspects of the Economic Growth of Nations II: Industrial Distribution of National Product and Labour Force," *Economic Development and Cultural Change* (July).

_____. 1966. *Modern Economic Growth: Rate, Structure and Spread*. New Haven: Yale University Press.

Lamberton, D. 1982. "The Theoretical Implications of Measuring the Communication Sector," in Lamberton, D. and Jussawalla, M., *Communication Economics and Development*. New York: Pergamon Press.

Lamberton, D., and Jussawalla, M. 1982. "Communication Economics and Development: An Economics of Information Perspective," in Lamberton, D., and Jussawalla, M., *Communication Economics and Development*. New York: Pergamon Press.

Lange, S., and Rempp, H. 1977. *Qualitative and Quantitative Aspects of the Information Sector*. Karlsruhe: Karlsruhe Institut fur Systemtechnik und Innovationsforschung.

Lazarsfeld, P., and Kendall, P. 1960. "The Communications Behavior of the Average American," in Schramm, W. (ed.), *Mass Communications*. Chicago: University of Illinois Press.

Leichter, H. 1983. "The Patterns and Origins of Policy Diffusion: The Case of the Commonwealth," *Comparative Politics* (January):223-33.

Lerner, D. 1958. *The Passing of Traditional Societies*. Glenco, Ill.: Free Press.

_____. 1963. "Towards a Communication Theory of Modernization: A Set of Considerations," in Pye, L. (ed.), *Conference on Communications and Development*. Princeton, N.J.: Princeton University Press.

_____. 1976. "Towards a New Paradigm," in Lerner, D., and Schramm, W. (eds.), *Communication and Change: The Past Ten Years and the Next*. Honolulu: University Press of Hawaii.

Linder, S. B. 1961. *An Essay in Trade and Transformation*. New York: Wiley.

Lindblom, C.E. 1977. *Politics and Markets*. New York: Basic Books.

McClelland, D. 1961. *The Achieving Society*. Princeton, N.J.: Van Nostrand.

McCronne, D., and Cnudde, C. 1967. "Towards a Communications Theory of Democratic Political Development: A Causal Model," *American Political Science Review* 61.

Machlup, F. 1962. *The Production and Distribution of Knowledge in the United States*. Princeton, N.J.: Princeton University Press.

McVoy, E. 1940. "Patterns of Diffusion in the United States," *American Sociological Review* 5 (April):219–27.

Maine, M.J.S. 1885. *Popular Government*. London: Murray.

Majumdar, B. 1982. *Innovations, Product Development and Technology Transfers: An Empirical Study of Dynamic Competitive Advantage*. Washington, D.C.: University Press of America.

Mansfield, E. 1968. *Industrial Research and Technological Innovation*. New York: W. W. Norton.

Marsch, D. 1976. "Telecommunications as a Factor in the Economic Development of a Country," *IEEE Transactions on Communications* 24 (July).

Marx, K. and Engels, F. 1969. *Selected Works*. Moscow: Progress.

Middleton, K., and Jussawalla, M. 1981. *The Economics of Communication: A Selected Bibliography with Abstracts*. New York: Pergamon Press.

M.I.T. 1982. *Conference on the Measurement of Communication Flows*, Wellesley College, Wellesley, Mass.: July 27-30.

Modelski, G. 1978. "The Long Cycle of Global Politics and the Nation-State," *Comparative Studies in Social History* 20:214–35.

Montamaneix, M. G. 1974. *Le Téléphone*. Paris: Presses Universitaires de France.

Musgrave, R. A. 1969. *Fiscal Systems*. New Haven: Yale University Press.

Nettl, J. 1968. "The State as a Conceptual Variable," *World Politics* 20 (July):559–92.

Nordlinger, E. 1984. *Theorizing the State: Autonomy and Support*. Paper presented at the Joint Seminar on Political Development, Harvard-M.I.T.

OECD. 1981. *Information Activities, Electronics and Telecommunications Technologies*. Paris: OECD.

Parker, E., and Porat, M. U. 1975. *Social Implications of Computer/Telecommunications Systems*. Paper presented at the Conference on Computer/Telecommunications Policies, Paris, February.

Parker, I. 1981. "Innis, Marx and the Economics of Communication: A Theoretical Aspect of Canadian Political Economy," in Melody, W., et al., *Culture, Communication and Dependency: The Tradition of H. A. Innis*. Norwood, N.J.: Ablex.

Paul, S. 1985. *Choosing between Private and Public Alternatives in Development: Criteria, Constraints and Challenges*. World Bank: Mimeographed.

Pavit, I. K., and Wald, S. 1971. *The Conditions for Success in Technological Innovation*. Paris: OECD.

Peacock, A. R., and Wiseman, J. 1967. *The Growth of Public Expenditure in the United Kingdom*. London: Allen and Unwin.

Perry, C. 1977. "The British Experience 1876-1912: The Impact of the Telephone during the Years of Delay," in Pool, I. de Sola (ed.), *The Social Impact of the Telephone*. Cambridge, Mass.: The M.I.T. Press.

Perry, J., and Kraemer, K. 1979. *Technological Innovation in American Local Governments: The Case of Computing*. New York: Pergamon Press.

Pfeffer, J., and Leblevici, H. 1977. "Information Technology and Organizational Structure," *Pacific Sociological Review* 20:241–61.

Pierce, W., and Jequier, N. 1982. *Telecommunications and Development: General Synthesis Report on the Contribution of Telecommunications to Economics and Social Development*. Geneva and Paris: ITU/OECD.

Pool, I. de Sola. 1963. "The Mass Media and Politics in the Modernization Process," in
    Pye, L. (ed.), *Conference on Communications and Development*. Princeton, N.J.:
    Princeton University Press.
_____. 1973. "Communication Systems," in Pool, I. de Sola (ed.), *Handbook of
    Communication*. Chicago: Rand McNally.
Pool, I. de Sola, Inose, H., Takasaki, N., and Hurwitz, R. 1984. *Census of Communication
    Flows*. Amsterdam: North Holland Publishing. Reprinted with permission of
    North-Holland Publishing (Amsterdam).
Porat, M. U. 1975. *Defining an Information Sector in the U.S. Economy*. Program in
    Information Technology and Telecommunications Report No. 15, Stanford
    University.
_____. 1976. *The Information Economy*. Unpublished Ph.D. dissertation, Stanford
    University.
_____. 1977. *The Information Economy*. Washington, D.C.: U.S. Department of
    Commerce, Office of Telecommunications.
Porter, M. 1980. *Competitive Strategy*. New York: Free Press.
Price, D. 1965. *The Scientific State*. Cambridge, Mass.: Harvard University Press.
Pye, L. 1963. *Communication and Development*. Princeton, N.J.: Princeton University
    Press.
Rada, J. 1981. *The Impact of Microelectronics and Information Technology with Case
    Studies in Latin America*. Unpublished report, UNESCO.
Rogers, E., and Shoemaker, F. 1971. *Communication of Innovation*. New York: Free
    Press.
Rokkan, S. 1973. "Cities, States and Nations: A Dimensional Model for the Study of
    Contrasts in Development," in Eisenstadt, S., and Rokkan, S. (eds.), *Building
    States and Nations*. Beverly Hills, Calif.: Sage.
_____. 1980. "Territories, Centres, and Peripheries: Towards a Geoethnic-
    Geoeconomic-Geopolitical Model of Differentiation within Western Europe," in
    Gottman, J. (ed.), *Centre and Periphery: Spatial Variations in Politics*. Beverly
    Hills, Calif.: Sage.
Rose, R. 1976. "On the Priorities of Government: A Developmental Analysis of Public
    Policies," *European Journal of Political Research* 4:321-50.
Russett, B. 1963. *Community and Contention: Britain and America in the Twentieth
    Century*. Cambridge, Mass.: M.I.T. Technology Press.
Russett, B., Alker, H., Deutsch, K., and Laswell, H. 1964. *World Handbook of Political
    and Social Indicators*. New Haven: Yale University Press.
Sabolo, Y., Gaude, J., and Wery, R. 1975. *The Service Industries*. Geneva: ILO.
Saito, T., Inose, H., and Kageyama, S. 1983. "A Comparative Study of the Mode of
    Domestic and Transborder Information Flows, including Data," *Information
    Economics and Policy* 1:75-92.
Saunders, R., Warford, J., and Wellenius, B. 1983. *Telecommunications and Economic
    Development*. Baltimore: Johns Hopkins University Press.
Schapiro, P. 1976. "Telecommunications and Industrial Development," *IEEE Trans-
    actions on Communications* 24 (March).
Schmitter, P., Coatsworth, J., and Przeworski, J. 1979. "Historical Perspectives on the State,
    Civil Society and the Economy in Latin America." Prolegomenon to a workshop at
    the University of Chicago, 1976-77, mimeographed, as quoted by Oszlak, O.
    (1982). *La Formación del Estado Argentino*. Buenos Aires: Editorial de Belgrano.

Schramm, W. 1964. *Mass Media and National Development*. Stanford, Calif.: Stanford University Press.

Schramm, W., and Ruggels, W. 1967. "How Mass Media Systems Grow," in Lerner, D., and Schramm, W., *Communication and Change in Developing Countries*. Honolulu: East-West Center Press.

Sharkansky, I. 1970. *Regionalism in American Politics*. New York: Bobbs-Merrill.

Shils, E. 1975. *Center and Periphery*. Chicago: University of Chicago Press.

Short, J., Williams, E., and Christie, B. 1976. *The Social-Psychology of Telecommunications*. London: John Wiley and Sons.

Singelmann, J. 1978. *From Agriculture to Services*. Beverly Hills, Calif.: Sage.

Skocpol, T. 1979. *States and Social Revolutions*. New York: Cambridge University Press. Excerpts reprinted with permission.

Slack, J. 1984. *Communication Technologies and Society: Conceptions of Causality and the Politics of Technological Intervention*. Norwood, N.J.: Ablex.

Snow, M. 1986. *Marketplace for Telecommunications: Regulation and Deregulation in Industrialized Democracies*. New York: Longman.

Socol, S. 1977. "COMSAT's First Decade—Difficulties In Interpreting The Communications Satellite Act of 1962," *Georgia Journal of International And Comparative Law*, 7:678–692.

Stigler, G. 1961. "The Economics of Information," *The Journal of Political Economy* 69:213–25.

Stoneman, P. 1976. "Technological Diffusion and the Computer Revolution, the U.K. Experience." Department of Applied Economics Monograph 25, Cambridge University.

Strassoldo, R. 1980. "Centre-Periphery and System-Boundary: Culturological Perspectives," in Gottman, J. (ed.), *Centre and Periphery: Spatial Variations in Politics*. Beverly Hills, Calif.: Sage.

Taborsky, M. 1960. "Madagascar: Development and Social Mobilization," as quoted by Deutsch, K., "Transaction Flows as Indicators of Social Cohension," in Jacob, P., and Toscano, J., *The Integration of Political Communities*. Philadelphia: University of Pennsylvania.

Taylor, C. L. (ed.). 1968. *Aggregate Data Analysis: Political and Social Indicators in Cross-National Research*. Report of the International Social Science Council. Paris: Mouton.

————— (ed.). 1983. *Why Governments Grow: Measuring Public Sector Size*. Beverly Hills, Calif.: Sage.

Telser, L. 1973. "Searching for the Lowest Price," *American Economic Journal* 63 (May):40–51.

Thomas, G. M., and Meyer, J. 1980. "Regime Changes and State Power in an Intensifying World State System," in Bergensen, A. (ed.), *Studies of the Modern World-System*. New York: Academic Press.

Thomas, G. M., Ramirez, F. O., Meyer, J. W., and Gobalet, J. 1979. "Maintaining National Boundaries in the World System: The Rise of Centralist Regimes," in Meyer, J., and Hannan, M. (eds.), *National Development and the World System*. Chicago: University of Chicago Press.

Thompson, J. 1967. *Organizations in Actions*. New York: McGraw-Hill.

Tilton, J. 1971. *International Diffusion of Technology: The Case of Semiconductors*. Washington, D.C.: Brookings Institution.

Toennies, F. 1971. *On Sociology: Pure, Applied and Empirical*. Chicago: University of Chicago Press.

Tomita, J. 1975. *Information Census Flow*. Ministry of Posts and Telecommunications, Tokyo.

UNESCO. Division of Statistics on Culture and Communication. 1979. *Statistics on Radio and Television 1960–1976*. Paris: UNESCO.

_____. 1982. *Cultural Statistics and Cultural Development*. Report No. CSR-C-27. Paris: UNESCO.

Uno, K. 1982. "The Role of Communications in Economic Development: The Japanese Experience," in Jussawalla, M., and Lamberton, D. M. (eds.), *Communication Economics and Development*. Elmsford, N.Y.: Pergamon Press.

UPU (Universal Postal Union). 1971. *Postal Market Research*. Bern: International Bureau of the UPU.

Vitro, R. 1984. *The Information Sector: A Crossroad for Development*. Presentation at the Transnational Data Reporting Service, Face-to-Face Session No. 10, 21 May.

Von Thuenen, F. 1966. *The Isolated State*, as quoted by Gottman, J., "Confronting Centre and Periphery," in Gottman, J. (ed.), *Centre and Periphery: Spatial Variations in Politics*. Beverly Hills, Calif.: Sage.

Walker, J. L. 1969. "The Diffusion of Innovations among American States," *American Political Science Review* 63:880–99.

Wall, S. D. 1977. *Four Sector Time Series of the U.K. Labour Force 1841–1971*. London: U.K. Post Office, Long Range Studies Division.

Warner, K. E. 1974."The Need for Some Innovative Concepts of Innovation: An Examination of Research on the Diffusion of Innovations," *Policy Sciences* 5:433–51.

Webb, E., and Campbell, D. 1973. "Experience on Communication Effects," in Pool, I. de Sola (ed.), *Handbook of Communication*. Chicago: Rand McNally.

Weber, M. 1946. "Wirtschaft und Gesellschaft," in Gerth, M., and Mills, C., *From Max Weber: Essays in Sociology*. New York: Oxford University Press.

_____. 1971. *Economie et Société* (2 vol.). Paris: Plon.

Wells, L. 1972. *The Product Life Cycle and International Trade*. Boston: Harvard University Graduate School Of Business Administration.

Wiener, N. 1948. *Cybernetics*. New York: Wiley.

World Bank. (1982). *World Development Report*. New York: Oxford University Press.

# Index

# About the Author

RAUL LUCIANO KATZ is a consultant specializing in strategic applications and management of information technologies, with Booz, Allen & Hamilton, Inc.

Prior to joining Booz Allen, Dr. Katz worked for the Chase Manhattan Bank's International Operations and Systems Group. He joined Chase after serving as a consultant to the United Nations, UNESCO, and the Argentine and French governments.

Dr. Katz holds a Ph.D. in political science and management and an M.S. in political science, both from the Massachusetts Institute of Technology. He also received a *Licence* and a *Maîtrise* in information sciences from the University of Paris-II, as well as a *Licence* in history and a *Maîtrise* in political science from the University of Paris-Sorbonne.

Dr. Katz has published articles in *Telecommunications Policy* and *The Information Society*. His doctoral dissertation was awarded the 1986 K. Kyoon Hur Memorial Dissertation Award from the International Communications Association. He has lectured on several topics, including information systems planning, the economic impact of information systems, the use of decision support systems, and industrial policy in the information field.

Dr. Katz was born in Buenos Aires. He grew up in Argentina, and currently resides in New York City.